Lost Restaurants
OF
PORTLAND, OREGON

Lost Restaurants OF PORTLAND, OREGON

THERESA GRIFFIN KENNEDY

AMERICAN PALATE

Published by American Palate
A Division of The History Press
Charleston, SC
www.historypress.com

Front cover images: Exterior image of the Club 21. © *Thomas Robinson*; Horst Mager cooking for the camera. *Courtesy of Joel Hamberg*; the Centennial Queen, circa 1959. *Courtesy of Doug Roylance*; early exterior shot of Thiele's. © *Thomas Robinson*.

Back cover images: QP's on a typical busy day, circa 1980s. *Courtesy of Herb Swanson*; a full restaurant. *Courtesy of Joel Hamberg*.

First published 2022

Manufactured in the United States

ISBN 9781467143301

Library of Congress Control Number: 2022937934

Notice: The information in this book is true and complete to the best of our knowledge. It is offered without guarantee on the part of the author or The History Press. The author and The History Press disclaim all liability in connection with the use of this book.

I dedicate this book to my father, Dorsey Edwin Griffin, also a writer and author. My father was the kindest, gentlest and hardest-working man I ever knew—may he rest in peace. To my mother, Doris Anna MacDougal Griffin, outspoken leader, dedicated Earth mother and the hardest-working woman I've ever known. To my precious daughter, Amelia Kennedy, a beautiful tough cookie with a heart of gold. And lastly to my precious and irreplaceable siblings:

Dennis Griffin
Margaret Griffin (RIP)
Brendan Griffin
Bernard Griffin
Marcia Griffin
Mary Griffin (RIP)
Brongaene Griffin
Galen Griffin

As well as my beloved nephews and nieces:

Rudy Alex Bunn (RIP angel!)
Justin Griffin
Chelsea Griffin
Audrey Griffin
Jacob Hinsvark
Carly Peterson
Nicholas Griffin

Portland is often seen as a sheltered Waldorf child in a mossy fairy-tale world of chanterelles and huckleberries; a quaint village populated by trust-fund wunderkinds who run food carts, each serving something more precious than the last. But Portland's culinary history actually tells a different story: the tales of the salmon-people, the pioneers and immigrants, each struggling to make this strange but inviting land between the Pacific and Cascades feel like home.

—HEATHER ARNDT ANDERSON,
author of Portland: A Food Biography

Food has always been one of the strongest sources of nostalgia. The other life experiences that provide the building blocks of nostalgia may come later, but food always goes back to childhood.

—VIKRAM DOCTOR, *editor with the* Economic Times

Contents

Acknowledgements

The help I received in writing this book was provided by numerous people, each doing unique things regarding research and document and image collection. I kindly thank my acquisitions editor at The History Press, Laurie Krill, for her patient support and guidance regarding aspects of research, image collection and the gathering of important source materials and historical documents.

I thank my precious daughter, Amelia Kennedy, who recently graduated from Portland State University with a degree in history. I thank her for the ways she helped me understand the importance of historical context and how the book needed to take form and focus, as well as for suggesting I not overthink the writing of it. Amelia encouraged me not to ignore or gloss over the complicated racial issues surrounding restaurants like Sambo's and the Burger Barn. Instead, she suggested I honestly explore those issues head-on, sharing with me the importance of writing nuanced historical profiles.

I thank my husband, Don DuPay, also an author, for sharing innumerable details of Portland restaurants, details that might have been lost without his "oral history" involvement, including providing information regarding his parents' restaurant, DuPay's Drive-In Restaurant.

I thank the many Portlanders for their indispensable help, particularly the wonderful people from the "Dead Memories Portland" Facebook group. These wonderful folks, and others, generously helped by contributing artifacts, information and quotes on many lost Portland restaurants.

I thank Heather Arndt Anderson, George Alderson, Debra Hagen Baldwin, Joanne Broadhurst, Kerry-Lynne Brown and Michael Brown. I thank my dear friend Bruce Broussard; AJ Calhoun; Mike Ceccanti; Larry Cervarich; Stephen Chappell; Alison Chapman; my dearest friend from childhood, Rachel Clark; and Allan Claussen of the *NW Examiner*. I thank Tom Comerford, Robin Crandall, Doug Crowell and Lisa Cunningham. I thank Joni DeRouchie; Monica Drake; Pam Falcioni; Gena Fields; Sarah Gilbert; Katherine Sanderson Gray; my beloved mother, Doris Griffin; Laurel Gunderson; Kane Hannam; Sandra Hetzel; Brian J. Hunt; and my good friend and ex-husband John Lawrence Kennedy. I thank Roger Kofler, Scott Kruger, Kit Lewis, Mike Lindberg, Carolyn Luff, Anthony-Anton Long, Alex McNabb, Anna Mehrer, Corky Miller, Sara Alexis Miller, Sandy Moose, Barry Morris, Rosalyn Newhouse, Juli Norman, Darlene Olesko, Jim Pilcher, Lois Netherton Plunkett, Wendy D. Reusser, Darlene Richardson, Ken Rosenbaum, Kurt Ruckus, Charles Rynerson, Dennis Sellers, Helen Schneider, Tom Schrader, Courtney Sherwood and my dear friend Fred Stewart. I further thank Ken Soesbe, Herb Swanson, Perri Combs-Taber, Jeff Velasco, Dennis Vigna, Mike Weinstein, Chris Wegner, John Wilson, Richard Wilson and Cori-Ann Woodward!

For speaking with me personally, in interviews, I thank the delightful husband-and-wife team Steve Sander and Leanne Grabel from Café Lena, along with their lovely daughter Gina Sander. I thank former owner of the Old Wives' Tales Holly Hart for her perspective and recipes. From the River Queen Restaurant, I thank Diana, Pam, Chuck and particularly Doug Roylance, the adult children of owner Bill Roylance, for their wonderful assistance with photographs and other information. From the Hollywood Burger Bar, I thank the late Craig Elliot and his wife, Inka, for their feedback, photographs and memorabilia.

I thank family-owned Antoni's Greek Restaurant, Diner & Lounge, which also recently shuttered. I thank the Tzakis children—Anthony, Napoleon, Spiro and Katerina—for always making me feel welcome. I thank their father and mother, Denny and Helen Tzakis, the real powers that be, and of course the ever popular Nikolaous "Niko" Antoniadis, for generously allowing me to spend countless hours holed up in an out-of-the-way corner of their wonderful eating establishment. Having a place to go, to get away from the distracting stressors of home, is so important, and the Tzakis family made my time in their family restaurant an absolute pleasure.

I thank Val Ballestrem, education manager of the Architectural Heritage Center, for his help accessing information and records regarding the histories of various Portland buildings. Val's help was invaluable in the writing of the surprisingly complex profile on Club 21. I thank Fred Leeson, former president of the Architectural Heritage Center, for helping with specific information regarding the buildings that I wrote about in relation to the restaurants operated in those buildings. I thank writer and artist Lisa Flowers for providing me with her perspective and memories of the Quality Pie restaurant in a lively and whimsical remembrance.

I thank Steffen Silvis, an exceptional writer and journalist of considerable talent, wit and skill (who also works as a university writing professor), for giving feedback on several chapters. Thank you also for sharing your stories of restaurants that are included in this book—you are a treasure!

I want to offer my thanks to four outstanding men for helping with the most challenging aspect of completing this book: the task of image collection. I would like to thank Joel Hamberg for graciously providing *all* the incredible photos of Horst Mager's legendary Der Rheinländer restaurant from his private collection. This includes early and extremely rare original photos of Horst Mager going back to the 1950s. Your help in providing those images is so appreciated!

I would like to thank Portland photographer and collector Thomas Robinson for his gorgeous photos and incredibly kind assistance in obtaining scans of numerous photographs used throughout the entire book, such as photos of Manning's Café, Yaw's, Club 21, the Burger Barn, the River Queen and several other restaurants. Thomas made image collection on this challenging project infinitely easier than it would have been otherwise, and I am so grateful!

I would like to thank research librarian Scott Daniels from the Oregon Historical Society for going above and beyond in generously providing numerous photographs of early Portland, including images of the Monte Carlo and Henry Thiele's.

And lastly, I would like to thank Portland photographer Scott Allen Tice for all of the beautiful images he provided! This includes haunting photographs of the Lotus Cardroom and Café, Club 21, Old Wives' Tales, Sambo's and several others! To all these lovely gentlemen, I offer my sincerest appreciation. More than anyone else, the four of you made this book possible!

Introduction

Long before "Keep Portland Weird" became an expression that modern Portlanders were alternately proud or dismissive of, the city was infamous as a hardscrabble territory that eventually morphed into an elegant city of lights. Back in those long-ago times, Portland was populated by young, primarily male migratory workers with little regard for rule of law, the rights of women or the protection of children or animals.

In the early 1800s, the ancient land that became the Portland metro area was a forested haven. It was home to Native Americans such as the Willamette, Clackamas, Kathlamet, Chinook, Molalla, Tualatin and Multnomah tribes, who had lived peacefully for millennia, prospering and thriving. This forested land held mystery, danger and uncertainty for those brave enough to investigate its lush dimensions. One pioneer, Jesse Applegate, remembered what he saw when he came from Kentucky to Portland in 1843. At that time, he and his fellow travelers beheld a still untouched wilderness that would soon flourish with all the social complications and economic promise of any early American city, as described in his "Recollections of My Boyhood": "We were then actually encamped on the site of the city of Portland, but there was no prophet with us to tell of the beautiful city that was to take the place of the gloomy forest."

Portland's inauspicious start and rough-and-tumble reputation as a frontier settlement began to change when the "stump town" evolved into a city on January 14, 1851, after being granted a charter by the Oregon territorial legislature. When Portland was graced with a charter and the beginnings of

1 THE GREAT LIGHT WAY, THIRD ST.
Portland, Oregon

The Great Light Way on Southwest Third Street, from the Dan Haneckow Collection. *Courtesy of the Oregon Historical Society.*

civilization became evident (with the continued arrival of women), the city occupied less than three square miles of actual land space. Rather than the elegant, looming skyscrapers we see today, encased in reinforced frames of glass and steel, the landscape was newly barren and devoid of significant vegetation. What those early pioneers *did* see were thin smatterings of the remaining Douglas firs and thousands of rotting, desolate-looking tree stumps, which would later be eradicated with powerful dynamite blasts.

Most of the early buildings dotting the downtown and waterfront areas were hastily constructed hotels, storefronts, saloons and modest houses and cabins. Often they were so quickly thrown together that they were described as "slapdash," with some being no better than shacks. In those early days, the city had a thriving underworld community of criminals and predators. They blended in easily with the well-intentioned hardworking residents. The crooks existed in the open for the most part—a subculture of brothel owners, pimps, scam artists, prostitutes, gamblers and loan sharks.

With missing women, accidental maritime mishaps and rare occasions of murder blighting the Willamette River, along with the floaters drifting forlornly in the increasingly polluted current, Portland became known as the Sin City of the verdant Pacific Northwest. In spite of that bad reputation, good people from out of state continued to arrive in the hope of creating a better life, and the population grew.

After 1851, Portland became more active as a place of booming American commerce, with the silty waters of the Willamette moving steadily forward in silent evenness. The river, with its brilliant presence, acted as a constant reminder that import and export would define and flourish in this small, often violent port town. As the layover point for people traveling between

A photograph of what later became known as Stumptown. *Courtesy of the Oregon Historical Society.*

Fort Vancouver and Oregon City, Portland became indispensable to those early pioneers trying to earn a living and provide for their growing families.

By the late 1880s, leaders in the Oregon legislature had decided to build a port so workers with the U.S. Army Corps of Engineers could dredge the Willamette River. This would create a shipping channel from the city of Portland to the Pacific Ocean. The fact that those early pioneers built that deep-water port, with a water depth well beyond the requisite thirty feet, enabled the city to import and export using large, heavily loaded vessels. Each vessel docked at the pier corresponded to the load it was importing or exporting.

The dredging of the Willamette River is the primary reason Portland evolved beyond a wide spot in the forested tree line that, at the time of Jesse Applegate's visit, extended to nearly the edge of the river in a thick blanket of green. Without the dredging of the river, the city would not have been able to ship large quantities of grain, salmon, wool and timber products to such faraway places as China and Mexico. Quite simply, the Willamette River made the most successful industries of Portland possible. Such industries included timber, canning, shipping and farming, which became particularly active after another arrival, en masse, of immigrants in the 1880s. In no time at all, "The Clearing" became the busiest port on the West Coast, second only to the cosmopolitan elegance of the city of San Francisco.

The city began branching out in other ways too. Beginning in the 1870s, Portland began building the kinds of cafés and restaurants that would become central to the city's identity. This interest in high-end restaurants evolved over time as wealthier residents began building their homes in the hills. The southwest hills—or "the Hill," as it is still referred to today—have always been the choice location for the most lavish homes in Portland. All fine cities have luxurious residences on hills that offer the most flattering views of the surrounding valleys and city flats below, and Portland is no exception to that rule. With the arrival of working families from out of state, wealthier merchants and businessmen began developing property and purchasing land. With this growing trend, the identity of Portlanders began to shift, and an interest in appearing more sophisticated and worldly became more important.

Husbands and wives now wanted to dine in formal restaurants specializing in traditional and exotic cuisine, with fine china, flower arrangements and elegant silverware. As this phase in Portland culture began, so did the emergence of chefs and cooks from countries as far away as Germany, Sweden and China. Restaurants and cafés were quickly becoming important gathering places for the elite as well as the common working class.

One of the oldest restaurants in Portland remains open. It is, of course, Huber's Café, which is located downtown on Third Avenue. Huber's was erected in 1879 and was initially located on the corner of First and Morrison Streets. It was originally called the Bureau Saloon until such time that it was purchased by Tom Huber, who promptly changed the name, moving it to its current location in 1910.

Back in 1879, if a customer bought a drink, they also received a free turkey sandwich, which is what the restaurant still specializes in—the finest turkey dinners money can buy, along with one of the tastiest clam chowders in town. Huber's has been in the heart of the city since the restaurant business began, a rare achievement for any major city, and it is as beloved today as it was one hundred years ago.

But this book is not about restaurants and cafés that are still in operation. This book is about the *lost* restaurants of Portland—those establishments no longer with us, those special restaurants that we continue to remember and miss. This book delves into a familiar and universal nostalgia we can all relate to: the inevitable passage of time and the reckoning of the myriad losses that passage represents for each of us. The bittersweet memories of days out with our families, the sense of happiness and belonging we felt while dining out in some of Portland's finest and more modest restaurants, is the focus of *Lost Restaurants of Portland, Oregon*.

Like many Portlanders, I was fortunate enough to visit some of the classic restaurants that will be profiled in this book. The first restaurant I remember going into was a restaurant called Sambo's, located on Burnside Street. The atmosphere was family friendly, crowded and warm. The smell of good standard fare filled the air—burgers, fries and coffee being the main top notes. The cheap stuffed tigers near the cash register by the front door were a huge draw for small children, and on one special occasion, my father bought one for my sister and I that we were told we would share.

The booths that looked south onto Burnside Street were roomy and comfortable and upholstered in springy vinyl. They were situated one next to the other in a long row spanning nearly the length of the building. As a result, that section of booths was perfect for running back and forth. I remember my sister and me (after sharing our cheeseburger and strawberry milkshake) running the length of that floor, lost in the happiness of childhood.

At the time, I couldn't have understood why the restaurant would become problematic later or why of all the customers there, I remember only white people sitting in the booths and at the breakfast counter in front of the kitchen. Our visits occurred around 1970, so none of the larger significance of this particular restaurant would be understood by me until much later. It would be decades before I understood the sound reasons behind the restaurant's closure and the history of racism in Oregon that allowed it to be opened in the first place, using such an offensive and racially insensitive name.

In my life, I've visited a multitude of Portland restaurants, including the Beaver Café, the Carriage Room, the Chocolate Lounge (which later became the Orange Slice), Country Bill's, Club 21, Farrell's, the Georgian Room, the Greek Deli, the Gypsy, Hamburger Mary's, Henry Thiele's, La Casa De Rio, the Old Wives' Tales, Poor Richard's, Fryer's Quality Pie, Der Rheinländer, Rose's Delicatessen, Sambo's, Sam's Hofbrau, Sylvia's and many others. I never thought that I would come to see those establishments disappear one by one or that I would have only memories to associate with the great cafés and restaurants that were an integral part of my childhood and youth. However, I was lucky enough as a lifetime resident of Portland to have experienced the aforementioned establishments and the mostly delicious food they offered, along with their individual and unique ambiances.

This book will look into more than just the general history of various restaurants and cafés, detailing when they opened and in what cuisine they specialized; it will also examine the social and cultural impact those establishments had on the larger subcultures of Portland. People of color had to be affected in a multitude of complex and troubling ways by restaurants like Sambo's, the Burger Barn and even the notorious Coon Chicken Inn, which was once located on Sandy Boulevard, on what is now the site of Clyde's Prime Rib.

The histories of a select number of restaurants, their impact on the Portland community and how Portland benefited or even suffered as a result, including an occasional recipe, will all be shared in this book. I genuinely hope, dear reader, that you enjoy this short history. It truly has been, from my standpoint, a labor of love.

AUTHOR'S NOTE: Because of sparse historical information through public media, libraries or historical groups pertaining to Portland restaurants that have shuttered, some establishments covered in this book have fleshed-out, lengthy profiles with more details, photographs and even recipes for readers to enjoy. Other restaurants have modest profiles with less information, fewer details and no recipes. This is due to the difficulty in finding uniform levels of accessible information on such a large number of shuttered restaurants. I could not include all of Portland's most popular restaurants. I was able to focus on a select number of restaurants with enough available information to complete those profiles in something of an adequate manner.

Chapter 1

The Early Years

THE VEGETARIAN RESTAURANT, 1897–1909

One of the first restaurants to open in Portland was also the first vegetarian restaurant. It opened in 1897, and the sign on the window simply read "The Vegetarian Restaurant." This new eating establishment was owned by the enlightened Seventh-day Adventists, who were ahead of the times in terms of understanding the importance of wholesome food and how food is related to well-being and good health. They offered a different approach to healthful cuisine that began a trend in alternative restaurants opening in Portland that would span well over one hundred years. That trend would put Portland on the map as the place to go for some of the most exotic and unusual vegetarian cuisine in the Pacific Northwest.

The dishes at the Vegetarian Restaurant were prepared from vegetables and a moist, peanut-based meat analogue. Foods served at the restaurant included soups, stewed vegetables, fruit desserts, wholesome breads, nuts and berries. Located on Sixth Avenue between Washington and Stark Streets, the restaurant was owned by the Seventh-day Adventist Church and had a seating capacity to accommodate sixty-five customers. These church leaders were some of the first pioneers in understanding and promoting the connection between spiritual, psychological and physical health having its basis in adequate nutrition and a vice-free lifestyle.

At the time, the *Oregonian* wrote about the increasing interest in vegetarian food and restaurants in whimsical and sometimes conflicting terms. In one

The Vegetarian Restaurant in its early days. © *Thomas Robinson.*

such amusing article, titled "PROSPECTS WERE SLIM: Little Encouragement for Promoter of Vegetarian Restaurant," published on January 17, 1898, an *Oregonian* editor described a nameless man visiting the *Oregonian* to inquire about the restaurant business:

> *A pallid, wild-eyed young man with a starved look, called at the Oregonian office last evening, to inquire what would be the prospects of profitable business for one starting a vegetarian restaurant here. He was told that as far as the employe's [sic] of the Oregonian were concerned, his prospects would be mighty slim; that while they might forgo meat if necessary, a large amount of fish food was absolutely necessary to keep up the brain forces required. He said bran and middlings were much better for this purpose, and were used by the brainy men and women of today to make good the wear and tear of their gray matter. He went on to explain that there is already a fine vegetarian milk made and sold in this country; that butter is made from the butter tree, and that cheese can be made from peas, beans, etc. He said that vegetable perch and vegetable turkey are served at vegetarian restaurants, and by request gave the following recipe for vegetable turkey. "Two cups of bread crumbs, two cups of chopped peanuts, two eggs (turkey eggs preferable), two spoonfuls of diamond butter oil, sage, salt and pepper to taste, water to make very thin, and bake three quarters of an hour." The young man was told this no doubt would make a very excellent "vegetable turkey," and he could call next Thanksgiving when his scheme would be considered, but if he was busy he could put off calling until Christmas, and any Christmas within a dozen years would do.*

The crotchety *Oregonian* journalists were unwilling to consider the idea of a restaurant without meat, fish and dairy, and their ridicule of the unnamed man demonstrated that Portland was still very much a meat-and-potatoes kind of town—and that vegetarianism, according to the *Oregonian*, was nearly akin to witchcraft or at least something to make fun of and ridicule among the boys of journalism.

In another article, published in May of the same year, the *Oregonian* described the Vegetarian Restaurant as an eating establishment that appeared to be doing well:

> *ADVENTIST CAMP MEETING: A Vegetarian Restaurant Doing a Good Business. At the camp meeting, which was held in Salem, elders preached in morning, afternoon and evening church services, but it was the success of the restaurant that was the main topic of discussion. A novel and by no means the least important feature of the campmeeting* [sic] *is the hygienic restaurant operated under the auspices of the management....The bill of fare is arranged on a strictly hygienic plan, no meat or cow's butter, tea or coffee being served, and all cooking being done without the use of grease or butter. In the place of ordinary butter, the restaurant supplies a nut butter made of ground peanuts mixed with water and salted to taste. A health drink made from grain is served as coffee. It is well known that the Seventh Day Adventists hold the Sabbath, our Saturday, sacred, and are very strict in their observance of the day. At the restaurant yesterday, the patrons wrote their names on the meal checks and settled at some subsequent time. The Adventists display more confidence in the honesty of the average man than is usually observed.*

The Adventist approach to healthy eating included avoiding the dangers of exotic spices; all "flesh meats" were forbidden, along with milk and other dairy products, which they believed caused infant death by "Cholera Infantum." The Adventists believed that milk caused other forms of disease among adults as well, including gout, rheumatism, Bright's disease, disorders of the liver, myxedema and goiter. The restaurant also served a dish called Nuttose (later Protose, which added gluten to the mixture).

The food products Nuttose and Protose were created by the guru of healthy living, Dr. John Harvey Kellogg—the same Kellogg who rose to fame by making corn flakes a part of every hungry American's breakfast routine. Meat alternatives during this time were called "meat substitutes" and were invented by Kellogg, who worked as the head of the Battle Creek Sanitarium. The first meat substitute Kellogg created was called Nuttose in 1896; Protose came later in 1899, and both were based on ground peanuts.

Nuttose and Protose were sold and eaten as a canned meat substitute but somewhat distressingly resembled what we might recognize as the canned dog food of today. The restaurant offered vegetarian-based food for mere pennies as an alternative to the meat and potatoes common among hardworking Portlanders who felt that meat had to be a part of every meal.

In 1900, the owners of the restaurant published a cookbook called *The Sanitarium Eclectic Cook Book*, which featured recipes from the restaurant in an attempt to promote the idea of vegetarianism and a more healthful way of eating among Portland residents. Also that year, three other vegetarian restaurants opened in Portland, and vegetarian food became increasingly popular. Vegetarianism was changing the climate of Portland's food scene by offering residents more choices that might appeal to their moral sensibilities regarding nonmeat consumption.

In another *Oregonian* article, "Vegetarian Restaurant; Portland Eating-House Which Sells No Meat," dated March 28, 1900, the writer detailed another unnamed vegetarian restaurant that seemed to be doing well:

> The keeper of a vegetarian restaurant, which has been in business in Portland for about three months, says he has quite a large number of regular customers who never touch meat or fish under any consideration. He is doing very well he says, but his charges are so small that the better class of people avoid his place, thinking it has been established for the benefit of those who are hard up. And really, a glance at his bill of fare suggests the soup kitchen. "Soups 3 cents, dishes of various kinds 4 cents, and puddings 2 cents." The nearest approach to animal foods in this restaurant is eggs and butter. "Butter is not recommended, but my customers want it and so I have to provide it," the restaurant man explained yesterday. He has been a strict vegetarian for seven years, owing to a disordered liver prior to that time, but he feels well and hearty now. "I have only tasted meat once in those seven years," he said, "and that was a piece of Chinese pheasant forced upon me by a friend. How good it was! I could taste it for a week afterward and enjoy it. I do not think that man is naturally a carnivorous animal. His teeth do not partake of the canine, and his whole make-up proves that he was originally a root, nut and fruit-consumer. His meat-eating propensities have been developed in a state of savagery and humanity is now heir to a thousand ills in consequence."

What is interesting about the preceding newspaper article is the question of the morality of meat consumption in the last sentence. At the time, this manner of questioning the long-held tradition of consuming meat was highly suspect and often met with suspicion. But it indicates that many Portlanders were rethinking the role of meat in their lives and seeking alternatives even in 1900, based solely on the morality or immorality of meat consumption.

In 1901, Kellogg patented the meat substitute called Protose and described it thusly: "My invention relates to an improvement in vegetable-food compounds. It consists of combining gluten of wheat or other cereals with a meal prepared from peanuts or other oleaginous nuts. The object of my invention is to produce a vegetable substitute for meat which shall possess equal or greater nutritive value in equal or more available form for digestion and assimilation."

Directions for cooking Protose detail how it was prepared: "Wash wheat gluten until it is practically free from starch, then mix it with dry peanut meal in the proportion of 1 part of the nut meal to one or more parts of the raw moist gluten. To mix, pass the gluten one or more times through a vegetable shredding or other suitable mixing machine. Then carefully mix in the proper amount of water. Cook for 1–3 hours at a temperature of 212–230 F. By proper regulation of the temperature and proportions of the ingredients various meat-like flavors are developed, which give to the finished product very characteristic properties."

Kellogg went on to write in his lengthy document, "My product is purely vegetable in character. It contains no animal substance or extract. In color or appearance it resembles potted veal or chicken. It has a distinctly meaty odor and flavor. When a bit is torn off and chewed, it shows a distinct fiber."

One common dish served at the Vegetarian Restaurant after 1899 was called "Protose roast," which was prepared from the canned Protose and then cut and pressed between thinly sliced onions and baked. A sauce was prepared from mixing peanut butter, water and salt. Repeated basting of the Protose roast created a rich brown gravy. Cooking time, amazingly, was one to two hours. Also served were Croquettes of Protose, which indicates an early use of granola: "Form into croquettes, roll in granola, then in beaten egg, and again in granola. Bake until brown and serve hot, garnished with parsley."

During the 1930s, foods and recipes that were a part of the Vegetarian Restaurant began to be produced at the Adventist denominational sanitariums en masse, along with being produced by several smaller food companies operated by Adventist businessmen. The companies had operations in California, Colorado, Massachusetts, Maryland, Nebraska, Texas, Tennessee, Michigan and Missouri. In Portland, Lange Foods sprang up in 1950 and stayed in operation until 1968. Lange Foods was a one-man operation where Lange's Chops and other meat substitutes were made, using very little to no soy.

Each of the sanitariums had a whole grain bakery and special equipment to create meat substitutes in the kitchens. In those early days, the process was primitive, and technology being limited, the meat substitutes were based on wheat gluten, which is notoriously unpopular today for people who may have allergics to gluten. The golden age of this new wave in vegetable meat analogues spanned from 1895 to 1915, and many of the staff operating in each state had trained with Dr. Kellogg personally in Battle Creek, Michigan.

The foods were given to patients in the sanitariums first and then sold by mail order to other patients and finally retailed to residents in nearby communities. In rare cases, the foods were distributed regionally and nationwide. Through this process, thousands of people were introduced to meat alternatives. In time, the companies began to slowly go out of favor and ceased production because of competition from newer companies and additional governmental restrictions, as well as newer innovations in vegetarian food preparation.

Introducing the idea of an alternative to meat consumption for Portland residents with the appearance of meat substitutes began in 1897 with the Vegetarian Restaurant. Through the examination of historic newspaper articles, it is possible to trace a marked change in public sentiment regarding vegetarianism. What was once met with disdain became acceptable and normalized in Portland. The legacy of the Vegetarian Restaurant would change Portland's food history permanently, offering an alternative focus on dining with innovative and delicious dishes that were healthy but also, refreshingly, meat-free. In 1909, the Vegetarian Restaurant was bought out and closed by a local Portland businessman. Happily, by then there were several more vegetarian restaurants that had taken its place and would continue the tradition of vegetarian cuisine in River City.

MANNING'S COFFEE CAFÉ, 1916–1984

Manning's Café was first opened in 1908 by hardworking brothers Edward McClure Manning (1872–1956) and William Wayland Manning (1874–1938). Their first establishment wasn't really a café though; it was more like a modest coffee stand. The Manning brothers were the middle sons of four boys born to Melville Malcolm Manning and Delia Manning, from the well-known Manning family of Boston merchants.

Ed and William Manning were ambitious and determined young men. Coming from a merchant family, they were familiar with hard work and creative innovation. However, before there was ever a Manning's Café, young Ed Manning was finding his comfortable middle-class existence a bit restricting and wanted to strike out on his own. In his middle thirties, Manning took what savings he'd acquired and headed to Washington State in 1906. Once in Seattle, Manning wandered the city for about a year, looking for work and surviving with

Exterior photo of a Manning's Café. © *Thomas Robinson.*

help from his family. When Pike Place Market opened in 1907, Manning went looking for employment. He befriended a street coffee vendor at the market and asked for a job. Manning had learned quite a bit about the spice trade from his family and was a quick learner familiar with the import/export business, so learning about the coffee business probably wasn't difficult.

One year later, in 1908, and funded with $1,400 borrowed from his family by wire, along with other monies borrowed from "a dozen or so banks," Ed Manning opened up his own coffee stand at Pike Place Market. He began by selling his own blend of fresh ground coffee, which was roasted on the premises. To create a following, he charged customers two cents and four cents for cup samples, and before he knew it, Ed Manning had a large following.

Ed soon realized that this was something he couldn't easily manage alone, so he wrote home, asking his younger brother William to join him (this is rumored to have interrupted William's studies in medical school). After the elder Manning brother opened Manning's original location— the coffee stand in Seattle's Pike Place Market—they stayed abreast of their customers' desires and made every effort to comply with consumer wishes. When customers indicated that they wanted food and desserts to go with their coffee, the Manning brothers developed a menu that included sandwiches, sweet rolls and pastries. When customers began lingering while they savored their coffee and food items, the Manning brothers implemented a "café-like approach" to their coffee business with the addition of tables and chairs where customers could comfortably sit while sipping coffee and eating.

After Manning's coffee stand began to enlarge and expand, they changed the name to Manning's Coffee Café. Manning's quickly became known as a welcome respite for coffee drinkers who wished to get energized before work or just warm up on a cold blustery day with a cup of hot coffee, tea or hot cocoa. Eventually, the Manning brothers leased a space in a building near their coffee stand and fashioned it into a restaurant, giving customers the option of staying downstairs to enjoy a quick cup of coffee and possibly a pastry or going upstairs for a relaxing full-service meal.

After the success of their café in Seattle, the brothers opened a second café in Portland in 1914, with other locations cropping up across the country. The cafés became popular lunch and dinner spots for hungry travelers, and in time, Manning's became a nationwide chain with more than fifty cafés in a total of nine states. The logo for the coffee shops, which was painted on the awning of the buildings, read, "Manning's Coffee, fresh as the dawn!" and featured a painted sun, streaming with rays of cheerful light.

It is said that the Manning brothers created the tradition of the midday coffee break, incorporating the custom into American popular culture. A midcentury newspaper article from the *Oregonian* seems to confirm this: "Manning's still markets the brothers' special coffee blend, which originated the American tradition of the coffee break."

Back in the early part of the century, visiting the downtown area of any city or town was generally a special event for families. Life was simpler then, and the prospect of going to town to buy needed supplies, as many people lived in rural farming communities, held a particular glamour. People used a trip to town as the reason to do additional shopping, dine out and perhaps even search out some form of entertainment, like vaudeville, puppet shows for children or a silent film theater to watch the "flickers."

Having the Manning's Cafés located in the downtown areas of cities was part of their success and appeal. Customers who were busy and had come to town to run errands and have fun found that process was far easier with Manning's convenient locations. Whether their cafés were in Seattle, San Francisco, Portland or other areas, being located in city center was an intentional move on the part of the Manning brothers. They well understood that by being in city center, their businesses would enjoy better foot traffic selling the coffee and tea Manning's was famous for serving.

In an article, published in the *Oregonian* on August 25, 1959, and written by its food editor, Nancy Morris, the president of Manning's Coffee Company,

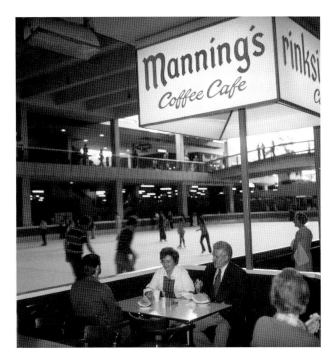

Right: Seating next to the skating rink, Lloyd Center. © *Thomas Robinson.*

Below: Interior view of the Manning's Café, Lloyd Center. © *Thomas Robinson.*

Andrew C. Glover, explained how to make the perfect cup of coffee. First, as he announced rather amusingly, "Coffee is a highly volatile substance. Its flavor, which is elusive, must be captured." Glover then explained that one must always use "uniform and measured quantities of coffee and fresh water." He noted the unusual response of coffee testers drinking fresh-brewed coffee from different-colored cups and how people tended to respond to clear, yellow, blue and small white demitasse cups. "It's psychological but invariably the tester will say that the coffee served in glass is too weak; in yellow and blue tastes funny, and is strongest and best in the small white demitasse cup."

Manning's Café was known for good standard fare in a relaxed atmosphere with white tiled floors and cheerful yellow décor. Favorite food items included its well-made cheeseburgers, Jell-O desserts, whipped cream banana cake, strawberry milkshakes, meatloaf, mashed potatoes and open-faced hot turkey and gravy sandwiches—all of it good American comfort food. It was listed as having five varieties of pie, three flavors of ice cream and pudding and six varieties of cake.

With increasing production of super malls in suburban areas, Manning's inevitably began to experience a decline in business and began shuttering locations. People became more interested in frequenting shopping malls, located outside downtown areas, and that included the competition presented by increasing numbers of fast-food establishments as well.

The original Manning's Café in Portland was located, not surprisingly, in the downtown area, but it eventually moved due to dwindling business. Years later, Manning's opened up two locations at the Lloyd Center mall. One full-service Manning's cafeteria was located on the third level, and a smaller sidewalk café was adjacent to the skating rink on the ground level. Lloyd Center was frequented by thousands of customers every day, many of whom worked graveyard shifts and on the weekend. By having two locations at the Lloyd Center, Manning's was able to maintain an active and successful presence in Portland, serving more than two thousand customers daily.

At one point, the smaller Manning's Café seating was directly next to the ice skating pavilion. Customers could dine while watching the skaters practicing their patterns, spins and jumps. While customers enjoyed a "continental atmosphere," the radiant outdoor heating system made it possible to stay warm while sitting next to the rink.

But Manning's was not without odd episodes of bizarre and unexpected excitement, from incidents of random crime to wandering wild animals.

As many restaurants are the focus of thieves on the prowl, Manning's was targeted numerous times by burglars intent on emptying the till. In early April 1957, the Manning's Café located at 6825 Southwest Macadam was burgled by men who broke in through a window and forced open several vending machines, stealing what money was inside and leaving a huge mess for employees to clean up later.

According to an *Oregonian* article, on June 16, 1978, at approximately 5:30 a.m., a two-year-old male deer was discovered by Lloyd Center security officer Rick Jones as he was patrolling the parking lot across from the Sheraton Portland Hotel. The one-hundred-pound animal had somehow made its way to Lloyd Center and became disoriented. Probably starving, the animal was being tracked by two Portland police officers and had first been seen by "unidentified civilians" at Northeast Thirty-Third Avenue and Oregon Street. The civilians chased it and were soon joined by the police. The officers explained to Rick Jones that deer occasionally came from the southwest hills, sometimes even swimming across the Willamette River and ending up on one of several Portland bridges in the relative peace of the traffic-free night hours, ultimately wandering the city, lost.

Helen Schneider of Vancouver, Washington, a grill cook, heard a loud noise as she was working in the Manning's Café next to the skating rink sometime after 5:30 a.m. After being pursued by the police, the animal had become frightened and had taken off running down one of the wide concourses within the mall. The deer trotted by the nearby Edwin Furnishings, past the shopping center auditorium and then turned south heading straight for Manning's. The animal was seen running at full speed as it dashed inside the restaurant, causing general mayhem and finally crashing directly into a plate glass window.

"I heard an explosion," Schneider explained. "I raced out to the dining area and saw the deer and the broken window. I saw he had been injured." Believing that the deer was charging her, Schneider was terrified, but the animal was merely trying to escape. "He sailed over the tables like logs in the forest!" she announced. The animal was finally cornered in Manning's all-glass entryway and captured by police. They wrapped the injured animal in blankets and carried it out to a waiting Animal Control vehicle. On the drive to Larch Mountain to free the animal, even after being tranquilized for the trip, the unfortunate deer died of shock as it had sustained serious injuries to its mouth and head. George Dobbins, manager of Manning's at the time, estimated the damage to be at around $200. The story was the talk of the Lloyd Center Mall and other area businesses for weeks afterward and seemed to confirm for many Manning's employees that *anything* could happen, and often did, in a restaurant.

Manning's served the food industry in Oregon, Washington, California, Utah, Arizona and Colorado. To make the food needed for all its locations, Manning's operated 4 bakery plants, 119 retail bakeries, 24 vending operations and a food processing plant. As the cafés began to lose business, after being relocated farther away from downtown areas, Manning's began to shutter more locations.

Despite this, Manning's proved to be adept at recognizing when change was needed, and by using incremental changes in its business, it made the adjustments necessary to embrace a modern and evolving world. Because of these slow changes and the loss of business, Manning's became involved in the institutional feeding field with food services to adapt to growing demands. Even in the early 1960s, when the restaurants were still going strong, Manning's was managing the food service programs at fourteen hospitals and was continuing to add hospitals to its list of institutions. Other institutions that sought out Manning's food and feeding services included nursing homes, colleges, retirement residences, factories and office buildings.

One Portland boy, Brian J. Hunt, fondly remembered his time visiting Manning's Café. While attending Benson High School in the early 1980s, Hunt would sometimes take an early Trimet bus over to Lloyd Center before school. After getting off the bus, Brian would walk the short distance to the Manning's Café and buy a cup of hot chocolate in a paper cup. With his hot chocolate in hand, he would walk to the edge of the Lloyd Center skating rink and watch the skaters practicing, all while he sipped his cocoa, continued to wake up and mentally prepare for his day—an endearing example of the innocence of a Portland student's morning routine, courtesy of Manning's Café.

In its heyday and even after it began its slow, inevitable decline, Manning's Café was a popular restaurant where people could rely on high-quality comfort food and an exceptionally good coffee blend, originally created by brothers Ed and William Manning only a few years after the turn of the century.

THE LOTUS CARDROOM AND CAFÉ, 1924–2016

The Lotus Cardroom and Café, located at 932 Southwest Third Avenue, or the building that became the Lotus, originally opened as Hotel Albion in 1906. The hotel was a small, boxy structure constructed to the best standards of the day and built like a fortress. After being sold several years later, Hotel Albion was renamed the Lotus Cardroom and Café and opened in 1924. What people may not know is that the Third Avenue location may have been the second location for the Lotus Café. The first Lotus Café opened in Portland sometime around the turn of the century.

One of the earliest references to this first Lotus Café is from a 1910 *Oregonian* article titled "Ascher Beats Lawrence. Portlander Wins Opening Games of Billiard Tournament." Later, in 1914, a man named Harry Dreyfus was mentioned in another *Oregonian* article, "SALOONMEN UNDER FIRE," for "selling liquor in a saloon on the Sabbath and Bert Wilkinson [for] dispensing the liquor in the Lotus Café." The final mention of this first Lotus Café is from August 1916, when the same paper published the article "CLOTHIERS GET NEW SITE. Buffum & Pendleton to Occupy Old Home of Lotus Café." It describes the old Lotus in flattering terms: "The old home of the Lotus Café, famous for several years as one of the most luxurious drink

An early postcard of a Portland restaurant called the Lotus, circa 1914. *Courtesy of Theresa Griffin Kennedy.*

The Lotus on a snowy winter day. *Courtesy of photographer Scott Allen Tice.*

emporiums in the West, is to be occupied commencing September 1 by the Portland clothing firm of Buffum & Pendleton, according to the terms of a lease signed yesterday. The fixtures that formerly decorated the store at 127 Sixth Street, estimated to have cost about $35,000 have been removed and will be stored."

The ornate cherrywood bar spent several decades at the Lotus on Third Avenue and was created by the Brunswick Balke-Collender Company, a well-known bar and pool table manufacturer in Chicago. The massive bar traveled around Cape Horn in South America, then to Tombstone, Arizona, and then to a "whorehouse" in Aberdeen, Washington, before finally arriving unharmed to the Lotus sometime in 1927. The bar was thirty feet in length, thirteen feet high and believed to have been built in 1889.

When the Lotus opened in 1924, it began as a seemingly innocent soda bar during the height of federal Prohibition, which began in Oregon in January 1916. But even with Prohibition in effect, the Lotus began serving alcohol on the sly. Local Portland bootleggers were regularly getting into trouble with the Portland Police Bureau for selling illegal liquor to the Lotus. During those busy days of Prohibition, the working class wanted a place to unwind with a little booze, and they knew that the Lotus would deliver, either from its dank basement nooks and crannies or in the rooms upstairs.

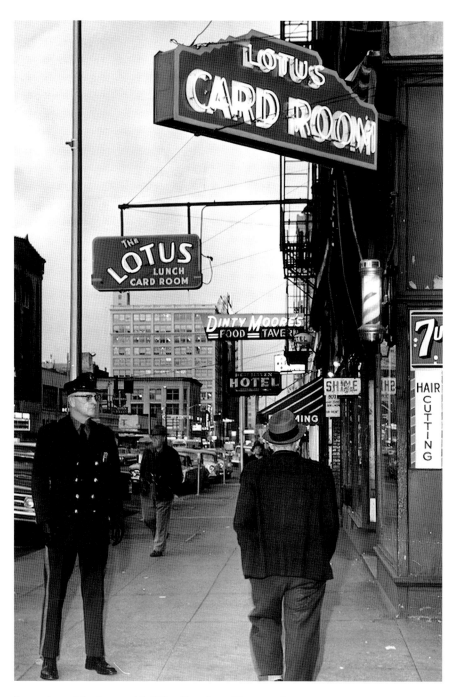

Street shot of the Lotus with PPB officer Gene Keck walking a beat. *Courtesy of photographer Scott Allen Tice.*

In 1933, when Prohibition was repealed, the back room at the Lotus, east of the main bar, became a convenient hangout for city and government officials. With city hall a few blocks away on Jefferson Street, this is not a surprising aspect to the history of the Lotus. Men would gather around lunchtime and often stay until after dark, eating, drinking and discussing the important political intrigues of the day.

The Lotus saw a lot of colorful history in its more than nine decades of operation. An old sign in the hall read, "Furnished Rooms 3rd Floor—Ring Elevator Bell." Much of the Lotus's history involved notorious crimes, including the open prostitution that resulted in women being assaulted, raped and occasionally stabbed over the years, with little penalty for those acts of cruel predation. As there was a discreet staircase behind the back room, near the cramped public restrooms and across from the old soda fountain, rumors abound that young women were kept in the upstairs rooms, sometimes against their will.

Long-held rumors contend that secret brothels were maintained for government workers and Portland politicians, and despite some protestation to the contrary, the stories of the Lotus and its connections to brothels from the North End refuse to go away. Retired police detective Don DuPay remembered when he worked the PPB Vice Squad that he often saw prostitutes entering and leaving the upstairs rooms during the 1960s through the southern-facing side entrance. Many of those women were then arrested for prostitution or the sale and use of heroin.

The Lotus had the distinction of becoming the first *legal* gambling site in Portland with an actual license. From the 1920s to the late 1960s, much of the clientele consisted of working-class laborers such as longshoremen, loggers, railroad workers, restaurant workers, hotel workers, street cleaners, gamblers and common street grifters. Many of these men entertained themselves twirling "dime-a-dance" girls in the smoke-filled rooms at the Lotus. The back room was open for card playing and gambling, and there were quite a few old-timers who still came around decades after gambling and poker had slowed down. Eventually, due to low turnout, any card playing at the Lotus ceased in 1990.

The food at the Lotus was never much to write home about during the early decades and was described as average during the 1950s and 1960s, despite it having a reputation for fairly decent steaks and what was called its "famous fried chicken." As the Lotus began to gain popularity in the 1990s as a trendy dance spot, it became known for higher-quality gourmet food and innovative alcoholic beverages. Popular appetizers included the

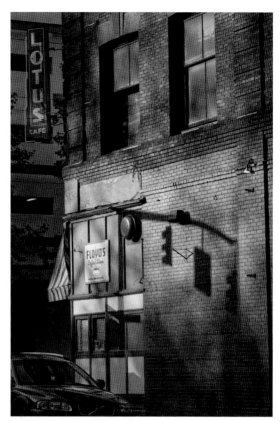

Right: The Lotus in a special light. *Courtesy of photographer Scott Allen Tice.*

Below: Interior shot of the Lotus, with the soda fountain in the back. *Courtesy of photographer Scott Allen Tice.*

Ultimate Nacho plate, the hummus and marinated feta plate, the spinach artichoke dip and the popular beer-battered onion rings. The Lotus was also known for creamy pasta dishes and generous salads made with the freshest ingredients.

Numerous employees over the decades have claimed that when walking down the steep stairwell into the noticeably dark and creepy red brick basement, they felt a presence watching them. They claimed that areas of the basement became inexplicably cold or that a cold shifting of air would imperceptibly drift by them when there appeared to be no logical source for the draft. Employees have also said that strange things would happen with the basement lights and electrical system. In interviews for this book, the author was told by two former Lotus chefs that the "ghost stories" are true. They explained how they felt the presence of someone watching them in the basement as they were gathering supplies, along with a sudden shifting of cold air, as if someone had quickly walked by them.

The existence of the "Lotus ghost" has many theories, but the presence is rumored to have existed for decades. Some think that the ghost is the spirit of a deceased Native American who is rumored to have been murdered in the basement. Some believe it is the spirit of a man who may have died in the basement as the result of shanghaiing. Others believe that the ghost is a woman who was chased from an upstairs room down into the basement and murdered. The truth is that historians will likely never know if those reputed murders even occurred, but those who have been interviewed have repeatedly stated that the presence of the Lotus ghost felt male to them.

The history that *can* be documented is that on the night of October 28, 1978, Thomas Joseph Lapari, forty-three, shot and killed Lotus bartender Cletus William Mitts, fifty-eight, after a dispute regarding how much Lapari had been drinking. The homicide occurred after the second and third floors were closed permanently in 1976 due to repeated fire code violations and general neglect. This was during a time when the Lotus had a notoriously bad reputation as a place where people got into trouble and where fistfights were not uncommon.

The jury deliberated six hours before reaching a verdict in the two-day trial, and while the *Oregonian* reported that the killing happened as a result of a simple argument on the part of Lapari with another customer, the truth appears to be even more bizarre.

Lapari was drunk that night in 1978 and began a loud argument with another patron in the restaurant. A former waitress/bartender of the Lotus, Anna Karns, in an interview, claimed that Lapari was indeed drunk and became angry when the bartender told him he would no longer serve him because he had become drunk and disorderly. When Lapari refused to leave, Mitts called Portland police, who later removed him. Lapari was described as a disgruntled Vietnam veteran who worked as a dishwasher and lived directly across the street in the run-down Hamilton Hotel, also reputed to be haunted (it would later come under the wrecking ball).

Lapari had threatened to kill Mitts several times while in the restaurant. After he was thrown out, he waited a few hours and then called the Lotus on the telephone. When he got Mitts on the phone, Lapari yelled into the receiver, "I'm coming over, and I'm going to blow your head off."

Lapari called again sometime later, and Anna Karns answered the telephone. Karns is immortalized in the book *History by the Glass* by Paul Pintarich as "a sturdy, red-headed woman with the unsmiling demeanor of a Marine Corp gunnery sergeant." Lapari asked Karns when Mitts got off work, and amazingly, she told him, "In about an hour." About an hour later, at closing time, Lapari strode into the Lotus with his arm raised high, holding a handgun. Karns remembered the incident in an interview: "I didn't know he was gonna *kill* the guy! But I thought *I* was done for! I thought he was gonna kill us both, but he didn't. He told me: 'I'm here for *him*! You get outa the way!'" Anna ducked behind the beautiful cherrywood bar as Lapari walked behind the counter of the bar and aimed at her co-worker cowering nearby. Lapari shot Mitts several times point blank, killing him instantly. After murdering Mitts, Lapari reportedly turned to another employee, perhaps Anna, and was reported to have said, "I just had to do it." Casually, Lapari walked out the door and strolled back to his room at the Hamilton. Police responded to the call at 11:24 p.m. and found Mitts dead. Lapari was arrested "a short time later while out driving in the area" and was charged with first-degree murder.

The defense argued that a charge of manslaughter was more appropriate, claiming that Lapari was "not behaving normally" on the night of the shooting because he was intoxicated. The jury and judge felt otherwise and gave Lapari a life sentence for what had been a by-the-book act of senseless, premeditated murder. The prosecutor, Paul Hurd, called the shooting "cold blooded, calculated murder." Lapari refused to turn over a weapon, and the police never did find the gun used to kill Mitts, so it could not be introduced as evidence.

The Lotus and the Rumor of Shanghaiing Tunnels

After the Lotus Hotel was demolished in 2018, the openings to three underground passages could be seen in the deepest parts of the exposed basement. The passages appeared to lead to other old buildings nearby that had been demolished decades before. Some in Portland believe the presence of these passages confirms that illegal "shanghaiing" occurred beneath the Lotus after the structure was built in 1906. Shanghaiing did occur in places like Portland, Seattle and California, but questions linger regarding the belief that tunnels beneath the Lotus were used in shanghaiing, or "crimping," as it was also called.

Oregon historians have indicated that there is no evidence to support the reality that tunnels beneath the Lotus were used for shanghaiing. The stories abound of turn-of-the-century kidnappers regularly seizing drunken or drugged men and transporting them through a network of lurid and dangerous underground tunnels beneath the city, some leading as far away as the waterfront. The victims were then allegedly sold to nefarious ship captains desperate for crewmen and willing to abandon every Christian value they had been taught in order to obtain those precious human bodies. The stories of shanghaiing tunnels persist to this day and have been immortalized by travel writers to lure out-of-towners to Portland for tourism.

Portland historians have found nothing in their research to confirm the idea that criminals used networks of tunnels beneath the Lotus to kidnap men for shanghaiing. That does not mean that crimes didn't occur in the basement of the Lotus. It would have been an ideal location for crimes and even torture to occur because the basement would have provided a soundproof location with lots of dark areas for discreetly storing unwilling human participants.

Portland historians cannot locate any recorded mention of shanghaiing tunnels prior to the 1970s. The rumors began, of course, many decades after the illegal practice was at its most popular and after it had, in fact, ceased. The type of historical evidence Portland researchers and academics normally rely on appears to be missing from archives and early police records, which would support the idea that tunnels were used in the practice of shanghaiing. These documents would include arrest records, police personnel files from the turn of the century and particularly those voluminous police ledgers, which were excellent sources for recording crimes and unusual events.

Shanghaiing did occur in Oregon, though. Crimps, like Joseph Bunco Kelly, would trick men who stayed at boardinghouses or who had passed out in bars, sometimes from simply drinking too much or from having been drugged intentionally. The men would wake up to find that they were at sea with no way to get back to their former locations. They would be forced to work as crewmen until they could escape at the next distant port. While San Francisco was the capital for shanghaiing, Portland also had episodes of this crime. The history of shanghaiing is recorded in Richard H. Dillon's excellent 1961 book, *Shanghaiing Days*, which details that illegal shanghaiing did occur in several states, including Oregon.

History indicates there were no tunnels beneath the Lotus that were used for shanghaiing. "It's not good history," claimed Jacqueline Peterson Loomis, who is the founder of the Old Town History Project and worked as a history professor at Washington State University. "It tends to obfuscate the real history, which I would argue is equally interesting and dicey."

With reliable history, researchers will find legal and municipal records referencing the digging that would have occurred between buildings and the intended purposes of such digging. "If there was something intriguing going on, it just boggles the mind that no one would see fit to say anything about it," said Richard Engeman. Engeman is the former public historian at the Oregon Historical Society and attempted to find evidence of the tunnels' connection to shanghaiing and was unsuccessful in his endeavors to uncover reliable historical connections.

If the tunnels under the Lotus were not used for shanghaiing, what were they used for? The earliest recorded tunnels beneath Portland streets were likely dug by Chinese merchants so they could conceal large quantities of opium. To purchase opium in the late 1890s in Portland and elsewhere was entirely legal, but the opium was taxed heavily. In order to get out of having to pay the tax, Chinese merchants would smuggle opium into their stores instead.

The Chinese also had large and complex illegal gambling operations that were hidden from the police. PPB officers and their high-up captains and lieutenants were not one to be deprived of their fair share of anything profitable, so the Portland police were regularly trying to shut down opium smuggling with their "heavy-handed raids by sledgehammer-swinging squads of bluecoats," according to the *Chronicle* of May 29, 2019. When this happened and "a half dozen cops suddenly showed up at one's fan tan parlor and started battering away at the door, having a secret hidden passage connecting the joint to a laundry shop a couple blocks away could prove to be quite handy"—and often was. The passages were still being used in 1914 as a place to store opium when Prohibition began. Those same hidden passageways became even more useful as a great place to store liquor.

The biggest change in maritime life that ended shanghaiing was the advent of steamships, which replaced sailing ships. Steamships were more effective, predictable, faster and far safer than sailing ships, which were more difficult to control. This process of steamships replacing sailing ships occurred from 1900 to 1930. As early as 1913, sailing ships across the country were having trouble finding crews, and the practice of shanghaiing had virtually disappeared. The Seaman's Act, which came into effect in 1915, also put a damper on shanghaiing. The law was created by Senator Robert M. La Follette of Wisconsin and Andrew Furuseth, who was a merchant seaman and an American labor leader originally from Norway. As a result of the new law, shanghaiing became a federal offence and fell out of favor even more.

So, is it possible there were men who were shanghaied, drugged, kidnapped and dragged into the basement of the Lotus? As the building was built in 1906 as Hotel Albion, it certainly is possible. But it is unlikely that there was ever any travel from connecting "tunnels" below the Lotus, as they simply didn't exist. There were rooms that resembled tunnels, but they had no connecting passages to other establishments and were used for solely for storage.

The Lotus was one of Portland's most beloved restaurants, with a history as spicy and colorful as its famous nachos, but its shuttering was just another example of the cost of progress at the expense of posterity and lost history. Instead of saving the building, which was as solid as a citadel and could have been renovated and converted to useful office space or art studios (allowing it to become a final nod to the historic tenderloin district), the building was sacrificed to the idea that old buildings are not of any great value and that new is always better, even when it's not.

Despite the Lotus being placed on the Historic Registry Inventory for decades, it could also be removed at will by the owner. The owner was then free to make whatever development arrangement he or she wanted, and this is exactly what happened. This occurred despite the fact that the old hotel was structurally sound and particularly beloved by countless Portlanders, including several prominent architects who tried to save it.

The shuttering of the Lotus Cardroom and Café in 2016 after ninety-two years in business was not just a loss because a popular restaurant bit the dust, or because Portlanders would miss the food and drinks, the fun atmosphere and beautiful, well-maintained first-floor interior—it was a loss because another historic building would be demolished. Despite public outcry that the Lotus was one of the last structures remaining in the historical tenderloin district, the building was sacrificed to the idea of progress. Another great piece of Portland history disappeared.

Advocates for the Lotus included the dedicated volunteers from Restore Oregon, who were the most vocal about saving and renovating the old structure. The group members attended meetings at Portland City Hall to voice their concerns and fight for the Lotus. They cited its historical significance and its unique and sound architecture. Unfortunately, Portland politicians decided against saving the Lotus, and it was destroyed so yet another mediocre high-rise hotel could be constructed in its place.

The loss of the Lotus and the role it played in Portland's rich history of restaurants, bars and turn-of-the-century architecture will continue to be lamented by Portlanders who care deeply for the historical significance of older buildings. The Lotus Cardroom and Café was once a legendary place where the men and women of Portland, sometimes hard-edged men and women, could gather together, eat, drink, play cards and enjoy life. The Lotus will remain unforgettable to the many Portlanders who loved it.

YAW'S TOP NOTCH, 1926–1982

When W.P. (Paige) and Grace Yaw opened Yaw's Top Notch in July 1926, the same year that the nearby Hollywood Theater opened, it started off modestly as a lunch counter and soda fountain with only fourteen stools. Yaw's first location was situated on Northeast Forty-First and Hancock just off Sandy Boulevard in the Hollywood District. Yaw's quickly became known as a fun restaurant with hearty burgers and a convenient drive-in that could be relied on for great service by cheerful staff.

As one of Portland's longest-running eateries, Yaw's fed multiple generations of eastside Portlanders and became known as the place to be seen, becoming especially popular with high school kids. The fact that Yaw's became the first completely air-conditioned restaurant in Portland probably contributed to its popularity during Portland's hot summers, along with Grant High School being less than a mile away.

Yaw's was famous for its big one-third-pound steak burgers, advertising, "We grind our own fully aged steer beef." Eventually Yaw's catchphrase became "The House that Hamburger Built." In fact, the popularity of its hamburgers prompted Paige and Grace Yaw to contact Franz Bakery and personally request that Mr. Englebert Franz create Portland's very first hamburger bun just so they could keep up with the growing demand for their "sandwiches." Yaw's was also famous for its rich gravy fries and wonderful

A night shot of Yaw's.
© *Thomas Robinson.*

berry tarts, often consumed with glasses of ice-cold milk, a favorite among children and teens. Favorite to-go items were burgers with a pint or two of spaghetti, which was one of its popular specialty dishes and made with a substantial marinara sauce.

Yaw's Top Notch had a variety of specialty dishes, including various spaghetti dishes, so everyone had a choice. There was Spaghetti Italienne, Spaghetti Italienne with chili sauce and Spaghetti Italienne with melted cheese, all of which were popular. Other dishes included fried ham with melted cheese on toast, baked beans and even a modest bread and butter side for older folks who liked it with a cup of hot tea or coffee, or children who wanted bread and butter with cold milk.

Yaw's was known for string fries, deep-fried pickles, chocolate pie, chocolate Coke and high-quality ice cream and milkshakes. It was also known to have served the first "thick" milkshake in Portland. One very popular drink was called the Green River, which was a lime soda drink, and it even had a Green River ice cream float.

On June 6, 1936, Yaw's Top Notch opened the doors to its new and larger location at 1901 Northeast Forty-Second Avenue, which was only a block away from its former spot off Sandy Boulevard. Yaw's ended up with more than fifty employees and, in 1941, added the carhop service with waitresses in roller skates gliding outside for curbside service for those busy customers (often parents with small children) or students who preferred eating in their vehicles.

Portland police officer and traffic cop Bob Svilar (pronounced "swiller"), also known as the "Tootsie Roll cop," would hand out Tootsie Rolls and chat

Above: Interior of Yaw's, with cook. © *Thomas Robinson.*

Left: Parking lot view of Yaw's. © *Thomas Robinson*.

with the Portland youth as they cruised into the restaurant parking lot. Svilar could be seen directing traffic in and around the Hollywood neighborhood nearby Yaw's, and he became a favorite police officer among the public, even giving Tootsie Rolls to people he pulled over for speeding.

Svilar was one of twenty-two Portland police officers who worked security for Yaw's, which could sometimes have the occasional bit of teenage drama, such as showing off by peeling out of the driveway, squealing tires, rapping pipes and even the occasional jealous girlfriend or boyfriend argument. Officer Svilar was a "people person" who loved to engage in conversation and had the rare ability to take care of business without making people angry. According to Don DuPay, who worked with Svilar as a police officer in the early 1960s, Svilar would "give you a speeding ticket and a Tootsie Roll and leave you smiling when you drove away, knowing you were still going to pay a hefty fine."

In all, Yaw's opened four locations in Portland and operated for fifty-six years, finally closing its doors in 1982. After a thirty-year absence from Portland, in September 2012, Steve Yaw, the grandson of original owner Paige Yaw, reopened Yaw's, but the venture was not successful and closed eight months later.

Steve Yaw was interviewed around the time of the opening of the last Yaw's, which was set up in a 6,500-square-foot space located at 1340 Northeast Halsey Street, with room for 140 customers, including 30 people on the soda counters. Yaw explained the nostalgia and allure connected to the phenomenal success of Yaw's Top Notch restaurants in Portland during the 1950s: "Cruising was an in-thing back then, and you didn't get tickets for it. It was all clean fun, and guys were showing off their hot rods and looking for girls. It was a good time in the '50s and '60s."

During an interview, Yaw revealed his admirable desire to re-create a lost time in Portland and his attempt to recapture that time. "The building was the right size, there's lots of parking—and we even have room for in-car service, just like people remember. Pull up, flash your headlights and we'll come serve you!" In the reopened Yaw's of 2012, the waitresses wore long pink skirts with white poodles sewn on the bottom front of the skirts, with white saddle shoes, just like in the old days.

Yaw also explained why the last Yaw's closed its doors back in 1982. When Portland city officials decided to close the Northeast Thirty-Ninth overpass, access to Yaw's restaurant was destroyed, as the restaurant was bypassed by traffic. According to Yaw, sales dropped from $8,000 per day to less than $1,200 per day, which was not enough to cover expenses and pay bills. As a result, that final location for Yaw's was shuttered in 1982 and sadly replaced with a McDonald's fast-food restaurant.

Yaw's will always remain one of Portland's cherished shuttered restaurants, one that created countless memories and even a few marriages. For Portlanders both young and old, the "House that Hamburger Built" was a home away from home and remains one of Portland's most popular restaurants, one that had its largest following during the innocence of the

Yaw's at night. © *Thomas Robinson.*

1950s and 1960s. It was a time of hot afternoons and warm spring nights cruising in convertibles as the sun went down. Boys in jeans and letterman jackets and big-eyed girls in bobby socks, poodle skirts and pigtails. For Portlanders of a certain age, at a time when the car was king, Yaw's Top Notch evokes the bittersweet nostalgia of a bygone era.

Chapter 2

A Growing Sophistication

THE MONTE CARLO, 1927–2000

The Monte Carlo was located at 1016 Southeast Belmont and became one of the most popular Italian restaurants in Portland. It was originally owned and operated by Ernesto and Emelia Ceccanti, who immigrated to the United States in 1920 from Tuscany to Portland to raise a family. In 1927, the Montecarlo Café in Portland was purchased by the Ceccantis and moved to Southeast Belmont later that same year, where it reopened as the Monte Carlo Italian Restaurant.

When the Ceccantis' only child, Elio, returned to Portland unharmed at the close of World War II, he entered the family business. Elio promptly told his parents about this new thing called "pizza" and encouraged his father to be the first to sell pizza in Portland. He explained that it had the potential to become a popular Italian food item because it was delicious and could be eaten with your hands. However, Ernesto didn't believe that pizza would sell and said no to the idea. It was only after the Caro Amico Restaurant, which opened in 1949, began serving pizza in 1953 that the Monte Carlo put it on its menu about three months later. So, while the Monte Carlo was not the first restaurant to offer pizza in Portland, it still offered an excellent pizza pie for Portlanders to enjoy that was uniquely its own, with its signature sweet marinara sauce.

The Monte Carlo continued in business for more than thirty years until the ownership and management was taken over by Elio and his wife, Lorie

The Monte Carlo on Belmont. *Courtesy of the Oregon Historical Society.*

Ceccanti. "The Monte," as it was affectionately known—or "Monty's" by its devoted followers—specialized in traditional Italian food of all kinds. This included extra-thick pizza, pasta dishes and steak dinners. Favorites were the hearty meat ravioli, veal parmesan, eggplant parmesan, veal saltimbocca, manicotti, seafood fettuccini and the all-you-can-eat lasagna and pizza specials. The Monte was known for its antipasto plate, spaghetti and meatballs, gnocchi, pasta classico, clam linguini, meatball sandwiches, tortellini, cannelloni and, for dessert, its spumoni ice cream, among other sweets. It was also famous for its excellent minestrone soup, which was a thin vegetable broth soup made from a simple old recipe Ernesto Ceccanti took with him from Italy that included chopped cabbage and slivered onions.

The Monte Carlo advertised a "plush" lounge area with live music. For many years, customers enjoyed the music of The Macks (Roy and Kay Mack), along with The Envoys (Bill Trevor on drums and Speed Anderson on piano). People came from all over the city, just to enjoy the live music at the Monte Carlo.

Fred Stewart, a Portland native and longtime real estate broker, remembered growing up and frequenting the Monte Carlo with his high school friends: "When I was in high school the Monte Carlo was one of our favorite places to go before and even after seeing movies, or just to hang out together. Their

The ceiling of Monte Carlo. © *Thomas Robinson.*

pizzas were big and incredibly tasty, even a pack of six kids couldn't eat an entire large pizza. They had all-you-can-eat lasagna and that meant *meat* lasagna with the most incredible sauce you've ever tasted. As a kid I was one of those meatball freaks so I was always going back for seconds and thirds."

Stewart remembered the high opinion his grandfather George "Goldie" Golden had of the Monte Carlo and its owners and staff. Stewart's grandfather took him to the Monte Carlo to celebrate special coming-of-age moments in his life:

> *My grandfather first took me to the Monte Carlo in 1979 to celebrate my start at Washington High School. He told me that the Monte Carlo was a special place and the people there were "Good people." That meant*

something to me. I always felt safe there with my friends. I have so many fond memories of the Monte Carlo. From 1979 to 1983, most of the major accomplishments in my life I celebrated with friends at that restaurant. It was where we went when they closed down Washington High School. It was where we went at night to talk about our lives and our futures. I could tell there was a lot of history there, just from the people who were hanging out. They were probably in their fifties and sixties. The women and men dressed up. The men wore suits and the ladies wore dresses and jewelry.

Stewart remembered the pride he felt when he joined the U.S. Marine Corps and how the owners and staff at the Monte Carlo treated him: "I went to the Monte Carlo the night before I left for the Marines. I had a large plate of their lasagna. When I got back from training thirteen weeks later, I remember walking into the Monte Carlo wearing my uniform with my friends. The staff was so kind to my friends and me that night."

The Monte Carlo was a place where celebrations were common, from birthday parties to anniversaries, business meetings, Christmas parties, engagement parties and baby showers. It had a bustling catering service for off-site private parties and a large buffet prepared each day with the choicest ingredients, affordable at a time when some customers struggled to get by.

Anthony-Anton Long, a longtime Portland resident, remembered going to Monty's for its lunches: "The Monte Carlo had a lunch buffet that was the stuff of dreams. I've still never seen a better salad bar. Tuesdays and Fridays were their lasagna days. I was so young and poor then, and they would let me get the buffet to go and I'd eat for days. When I first came in, the ladies told me I was too skinny and sent me back to get more food from the buffet. When I got back, they had wrapped a loaf of garlic bread for me, too!"

The owners and staff at the Monte Carlo were known for their generous spirit in helping those customers who were not wealthy. They were also known for their pride in Italian cuisine and in eating big. Richard Wilson of Portland remembered going to Monty's for the lunch buffet: "The cook [the owner, Ernesto Ceccanti] would load your plate with piles of lasagna and spaghetti, with a big ladle of tomato gravy. I remember one day in the 1980s I was there for lunch and the guy behind me in line asked for 'just a tiny bit.' The owner roared, '*This* is an Italian buffet and there are *no* tiny portions!' He then slapped a ten-dollar bill in the guy's hand and asked him to get his skinny butt out of his restaurant and go eat somewhere else. I laughed so hard I almost dropped my plate. Good memories at the Monte Carlo."

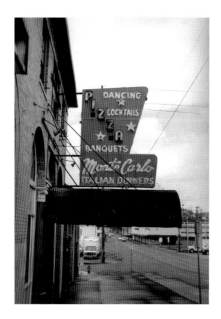

The Monte Carlo sign. *Courtesy of the Oregon Historical Society.*

Kurt Ruckus, also of Portland, remembered Monty's had a great dance scene during the 1990s. "They had a super hopping dance party there with DJ Mark Knight in the early 1990s. It would be in full swing from 11:00 p.m. to 2:30 a.m. on a weeknight. Even the Trail Blazers would show up. It was a total scene."

The Monte Carlo was created by Ernesto Ceccanti to serve the growing Italian population in Portland that sorely missed genuine Italian cuisine at a time when there were few to no Italian restaurants in Portland. The Monte Carlo fulfilled that desire for more than seventy years, but like all great restaurants, it came to an end. Elio and Lorie Ceccanti sold the restaurant in 1992 to retire. It remained under new management at the same location for another four years and then relocated to Gresham, where it lasted about a year before finally shuttering permanently.

In 2002, a devastating fire destroyed the building that had once been the Monte Carlo on Belmont Street. After a group of homeless people tried to light a fire in an abandoned building next door to keep warm, both buildings became engulfed; all that was left of the old Monte Carlo Italian Restaurant was gone.

Mike Ceccanti, grandson of Ernesto, opened up his own restaurant and named it Ernesto's in honor of his accomplished grandfather, the man who had started it all with the Monte Carlo back in 1927. All the same recipes used at the Monte Carlo, including the recipe for the famous minestrone soup and its special sweet marinara sauce, were carried over to Ernesto's. So, while the Monte Carlo was lost to time, the beloved dishes that made the Monte Carlo famous are still being made every day at Ernesto's Restaurant on Southwest Apple Way in Beaverton, Oregon.

HENRY THIELE'S RESTAURANT, 1932–1990

One of Portland's most beloved restaurants was the famed Henry Thiele's Restaurant, located at 2305 West Burnside Street, on the corner of Northwest Westover Road. The restaurant was named after its eponymous founder, Henry Thiele, who was the German chef who made a name for himself while working at the Benson Hotel as its chief steward.

Henry's opened in April 1932 and instantly became an overnight sensation with Portland residents and those from out of town. The restaurant became a visual landmark. It was instantly recognizable with its irregular shape, which was altered several times over the years with various additions, such as in 1954 when a wing at the rear was added along Burnside Street. When it was originally built, it was a much smaller building, as it was intended to be a modest sandwich shop. Soon Portlanders began requesting sit-down dinners, and Thiele responded by adding to the core of the building in the 1930s, the 1940s and the 1950s. The horseshoe-shaped restaurant with the booth-lined walls would become famous for its huge menu choices and its delectable desserts.

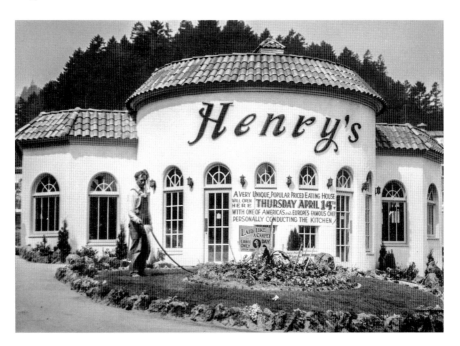

Early exterior shot of Henry Thiele's. © *Thomas Robinson.*

The structure was a stucco Mediterranean-style building with clay roof tiles and a semicircular, round bay at the east entrance. Other features included arched doorways, an arched loggia on the rear wing, vertical casement windows and a decorative ornamental garden with junipers and seasonal flowers. The location of Thiele's restaurant was significant. It was positioned at a busy five-way intersection on a wedge-shaped lot in the Uptown Shopping Center with numerous parking spaces adjacent to it.

The restaurant became an instant attraction not only because of the beautifully decorated interior, where Portlanders and out-of-towners could dine with family and be seen by friends and neighbors, but also because the restaurant provided the very best in hearty German cuisine. There was a cocktail lounge that was removed from the main dining area where adult customers could relax and have a drink in relative privacy.

Thiele's had the largest menu of any Portland restaurant of the time, which included a generous child's menu. Favorite dishes included the popular New York cut steak, southern pan-fried chicken, liver and onions, Eastern Scallops Sauté and the fillet of halibut dinner, among others. And no meal was complete without the house special dessert, the Princess Charlotte Pudding—always a hit, especially with little girls and their mothers.

Henry Thiele was born in Hannover, Germany, in April 1882 and educated in Germany and France, learning to speak and read French and English with the fluency of his own tongue. After leaving school at a young age by today's standards (he was a young teen), Thiele learned the challenging art of winemaking in southern Germany. From there, he learned the confectioner's trade for two years in Switzerland. Thiele's wide knowledge of cooking, winemaking and sweets preparation helped him later when he served as an apprentice to chefs in the Kaiserhoff, the Zoologischergarten and the Palace Hotel in Berlin.

In 1898, at only sixteen, Thiele was awarded a prestigious prize in a cooking exhibit, at which time he had completed only a year and a half of an apprenticeship. While other competitors had more than forty years' experience as chefs and confectioners, it was young Thiele who won third prize, an admirable feat. The confectionery exhibit that won Thiele the honor was an attractive Arabian scene of singular creativity and colorfulness that Thiele made from sugar, gelatin and food coloring. It is likely that Thiele used naturally created food colorants from simple things like beets, raspberries, paprika, saffron, blueberries and even concentrated coffee and tea.

When young Thiele arrived in America in 1914, he began an apprenticeship with the Waldorf Astoria in New York and later the Holland

Street view of Henry Thiele's. *Courtesy of photographer Scott Allen Tice.*

House to learn more of the restaurant business in America. He worked at the Edgewater in Chicago and the Francis Drake in San Francisco.

In 1908, Thiele married pretty Margaret Anderson, originally from Minnesota, with whom he had four children. Thiele had already worked in places like San Francisco, Chicago and Seattle, where he was chief steward at the Rathskeller, along with operating the Frye Hotel coffee shop, before working briefly in Canada. When Thiele arrived in Portland with his family, he set to work learning as much as he could about what seasonal foods Portland was known for—seafood mostly—and to create a name for himself.

Thiele started at the Benson Hotel in 1916, where his reputation as an excellent chef grew. He catered countless women's luncheons for groups like the Portland Women's Club, along with lunches and dinners for local area businessmen and various conventions. Thiele's menus at the Benson were known for their breadth and versatility, focusing on fish and shellfish, with excellent complementary sauces and, of course, Thiele's luscious desserts. Moreover, instead of being written in confusing French or German, which most Portlanders didn't speak or read, the menus were written in simple English.

In the early and mid-1920s, Thiele decided to be his own boss and began several ventures that, for one reason or another, were not successful. He opened a grill in the new Sovereign, a residence hotel; he took on the management of Simon Benson's new Columbia Gorge Hotel, near Hood

A family portrait with Thiele; his first wife, Margaret; and their four children. *Courtesy of the Oregon Historical Society.*

Exterior front view of Henry Thiele's. *Courtesy of photographer Scott Allen Tice.*

River; and he opened a large restaurant on Southwest Tenth Avenue north of Morrison Street and a coffee shop on Alder Street. Thiele even delivered box lunches on a fleet of motorcycles for a time, but ultimately after all these ventures, he ended up struggling to overcome serious financial problems.

Some time before the opening of Henry Thiele's Restaurant, Margaret died in December 1930, and Thiele had to regroup. Contending with the possibility of bankruptcy after the death of his wife, Thiele took some time off. But with the help of wealthy friends in the Portland community, Thiele finally opened his restaurant on April 14, 1932, which was also his fiftieth birthday.

The restaurant became a Portland legend, a place for the wealthy of Portland Heights and the elderly widows in the Nob Hill area to have lunch and dinner. Thiele's large European-influenced menu listed up to fifty dishes, including countless desserts, cakes, sweet breads and pies, as well as Thiele's own homemade-style pickles, which were set up to cure in the basement. The restaurant grew in popularity and had a seating capacity of up to 150 customers.

After Thiele opened up his new restaurant, he hired a young woman, ironically also named Margaret—Margaret MacDonald, aged nineteen and originally from Veronia, Oregon. Macdonald had been working at the Imperial Hotel when Thiele hired her as a bookkeeper. Eventually, she became a hostess and then a waitress, even learning to make some of the dishes. Thiele and MacDonald worked together for many years, forming a strong bond, and were eventually married in 1943. At one point during World War II, and with his second wife acting as the main supervisor, Thiele contracted to feed some twenty-five thousand workers at the Kaiser Portland and Vancouver shipyards. Despite being in poor health during this time, Thiele still operated the restaurant, but he had a bed set up behind the kitchen area so he could rest when he wished between duties.

During his heyday, Thiele became known as "the king" of Portland dining for both the Portland elite and regular middle-class Portlanders who wanted to dine out for a special occasion. Along with his famous Princess Charlotte Pudding, some other desserts Thiele was known for included the Bavarian cheesecake, a cup of custard with whipped cream, angel food cake, chocolate and white buttercream cakes, numerous berry and fruit pies and assorted coffee cakes.

Other savory dishes Thiele was particularly known for included smoked loin of pork with German red cabbage; bratwurst with sweet-sour lentils; lamb chops with bacon; baked oysters; lobster Newberg; chopped steak with mushroom sauce; baked breast of turkey; wiener schnitzel with anchovies; fried chicken à la Maryland; platters of deep-fried smelt; crab stew; Olympia oyster stew; and his roulade of beef, which was made from thin beefsteaks stuffed with dill pickle, onion and pork sausage and covered with a rich, tangy gravy. And there was his excellent Dungeness Crab Bombay in the shell.

James Beard, the famous chef who grew up in Portland, contributed two pages on Thiele's incredible cooking in his autobiographical book *Delights and Prejudices*, writing, "This man had a fawning manner and great ambition, but he was a great creative chef." Beard believed that Thiele's salmon dishes were his most popular and what he was best at preparing for his customers. "Thiele's salmon dishes were his true forte and became the feature of the Columbia Gorge Hotel, which Mr. Benson built for him. I can remember a whole baked salmon done with cream and fillets of salmon stuffed with a salmon mousse and then poached in a court bouillon." Beard claimed that Thiele created a reputation for "culinary sophistication" that made him something of a flamboyant early version of the celebrity chefs of today.

Thiele could at times adopt an imperious and unpredictable manner. In a personal memoir by Gerald Fisher, *The Scalawag: The Long Life & Times of Gerald John Fisher*, the author remembered working for Thiele's in the early days. Moving from Sellwood to a small apartment at Twenty-Second and West Burnside near downtown Portland, Fisher recalled some of the colorful experiences he had while working at Henry Thiele's:

> *With my experience as a cook, I walked into Henry Thiele's restaurant and met with the man himself—a short, stout man with a goatee and an accent. He told me the only job he had available was as a breakfast cook. I told him I could do that. He handed me an omelet pan and said "Make me a cheese omelet." I made it, rolled it onto a platter, put strips of cheese on top and slid it under the broiler. He was impressed. We always had five cooks on the line because at lunch and dinner people lined up at the front and back doors waiting to get in. Thiele employed sixty-five of us: twenty-five of us were kitchen staff, then three bakers, a head butcher and three helpers, four for the pantry, three at the soda fountain, one storekeeper, one wine steward, two fruit and vegetable preppers, four dishwashers and three janitors.*

Fisher has more interesting memories to recount in his memoir when he shared the drama that occurred in the day-to-day realties of demanding restaurant work:

Henry would always come in the restaurant in the evening. The big diamond ring he wore would sparkle and light up the kitchen when he waved his hand around. One slow evening in the winter, when the weather was wet and nasty, Henry took a tray of empty water glasses and accidentally dropped the whole stack behind a waitress. He screamed and hollered at her and fired her on the spot. That got everyone's attention. Later he went down to the dressing room where the girl was crying, patted her on the back, gave her a $20 bill and told her to come back to work the next day. It was not long after that when the counter was full and Henry came in and spotted a man at the counter with his hat on. Henry hollered from the other end of the counter, "You with the hat on! Why do you think we have hat racks? If you don't have better manners than that, eat elsewhere." The guy left in a hurry. I worked hard at Henry Thiele's and took all the overtime I could.

After Thiele's death on January 4, 1952, his young widow Margaret continued to manage the restaurant for several more decades with the help of her stepson Henry Jr. and Thiele's other three children, Margaret, Carl and Elizabeth. Margaret Thiele is quoted as explaining the continued attraction for Henry Thiele's Restaurant in a 1959 book by J.A. Armstrong called *Dining à la Oregon: A Guide to Eating Adventures in Oregon Restaurants, Featuring Famous Recipes for Specialties of the House*: "We are not the glamorous-type restaurant, but a solid family-eating place, and over the years have built our reputation on word-of-mouth advertising." Margaret Thiele eventually married August Petti, an Italian clothing designer who then acted as the restaurant's "suave and genial host" for years afterward.

Perri Combs-Taber, a Portland native, worked at Henry Thiele's during a summer in the late 1970s when she was home from college. She remembered a family atmosphere, a dedication to maintaining the large menu and the necessity of resourcefulness:

I worked in the pantry and had a good view of the whole restaurant. People came in daily and sat in the same spot. The pantry dishes were good and made fresh every day, as were most of the dishes on that huge menu. Margaret would type a long full page of specials each day. The cold poached salmon was so delicious. The lunches women ordered in those days were chicken salad, crab and shrimp Louie, or the fruit salad. There was a fountain where children could order sodas and sundaes. It was a little room near the kitchen with all the ingredients. Margaret would arrive with great fanfare each morning, with August behind her. They were usually loaded with an armful of flowers from her West Slope garden. She wore silk dresses and if a cook were indisposed she would roll up her sleeves, don an apron and get in the kitchen to cook until a replacement arrived. She taught me how to chop properly with a large knife. She said, "Don't chop like James Beard. He chops like a housewife!" She was respected and she earned it! A formidable woman and a role model to me. Also, the chicken salad was often an ice cream scoop of turkey salad!

Portland historian Richard Engeman loved the Princess Charlotte Pudding so much that after working a split shift as a young man at the nearby Roses Deli & Bakery, he once walked up to Henry Thiele's and ordered three to go at a total cost of $1.05. "Each was a perfect dollop of creamy pudding with toasted almonds capped with a rich red syrup. I wish I could still get one."

James Beard wrote of his love for the dessert, "And Thiele's Princess Charlotte pudding! I have tried for years and years to duplicate it, from the first days of the Benson, but have never achieved the same quality. It was rather like a fine *bavaroise*, but creamier, with praline in it and a supremely good cassis sauce over it."

Rachel Clark, daughter of two-time Portland mayor Bud Clark, fondly remembered family visits to Henry Thiele's restaurant with her beloved mother, Sigrid, and how much she loved the Princess Charlotte Pudding:

When I was a child, Henry Thiele's meant going on a fancy date with my mom and my brothers. Momma and I dressed in skirts, walking hand-in-hand through Uptown (the name we called that shopping area) and onto Thiele's on a nice Portland day. I remember being a little girl, sitting in the big overstuffed rounded booths with my mom and my brothers and ordering this treat. It was served in a little ceramic or porcelain dish, maybe four inches in diameter, perhaps with a scalloped edge. It was silky-soft, sweet vanilla pudding that was doused with a generous bright red cherry syrup with a few sliced almonds on top. I'm sure that these dates included lunch but I can only recall with clarity the Princess Charlotte pudding.

Henry Thiele's Restaurant was in business almost sixty years before finally shuttering in 1990 to the collective disappointment of many longtime Portland residents. The restaurant was replaced with a modest mall-like structure. Developers agreed to give Henry Thiele's one last nod by calling the new shopping center Thiele's Square.

Here are a few popular Thiele recipes:

Henry Thiele's German Pancake (also called a "Dutch Baby")

Makes: 1 pancake
Prep time: 15 minutes
Cook time: 30 minutes

INGREDIENTS
¼ teaspoon salt
1 teaspoon sugar
¾ cup all-purpose flour
¾ cup cream or milk
4 eggs, beaten
4 tablespoons butter, melted
½ lemon
Powdered sugar

DIRECTIONS
Heat the oven to 400 degrees. Start with room-temperature ingredients. Heat the pan—cast-iron skillets are best. Mix the salt, sugar and flour and cream. Beat the eggs, one at a time, into the flour mixture. Melt the butter in the pan (there is a special pan for making the pancakes, sort of a small, short, wok-like pan). Pour the batter into the hot sizzling butter. Put the pan in the hot oven. The pancake will take about 15 to 20 minutes to cook—it will puff up a lot. Remove the pancake from the oven. Traditionally, it was served with a squeeze of lemon juice and then sprinkled with powdered sugar. Serve with sautéed apple slices, tart berry jam or even fresh strawberries.

• • • •

Bratwurst and Sweet-Sour Lentils

INGREDIENTS
2 cups lentils
Ham stock
¾ teaspoon Henry's mélange seasoning (seasoned salt may be substituted)
1 medium onion, diced fine
5 strips bacon, diced fine

3 tablespoons flour
¼ cup vinegar
1 medium apple, diced
Parsley, chopped, for garnish

DIRECTIONS
Soak lentils in cold water for 2 hours. Drain and cover with ham stock. Add mélange seasoning and simmer until three quarters done. Drain, retaining the liquid. Sauté onion and bacon. Blend in flour and cook slowly until golden brown. Add vinegar and cook until thickened. Add apples and lentils and simmer slowly until done. Serve with bratwurst (sausage), garnished with chopped parsley. Serves 4.

To prepare the bratwurst, put enough water in saucepan to cover the bratwurst and steam slowly for ten minutes. Be sure not to let boil. Remove bratwurst and place in skillet with sliced onion and butter. Sauté to a light brown and serve with sweet-sour lentils.

• • • •

Henry Thiele's Bearnaise Sauce (makes 1 cup)

INGREDIENTS
½ cup (118 milliliters) dry white wine
4 shallots, finely sliced
2 tablespoons (30 grams) fresh tarragon
8 tablespoons (113 grams) unsalted butter
4 egg yokes
Salt to taste

DIRECTIONS
Reduce the white wine, shallots and tarragon in a saucepan over medium heat, until there is a thick glaze at the bottom of the saucepan, being sure not to let it burn. In a separate pan, melt the butter until it begins to bubble. In a large bowl, beat together the egg yolks and then add the wine glaze and the butter, beating until it's thickened and emulsified, almost the consistency of mayonnaise (this can be done in the food processor). Season with salt and serve.

• • • •

Henry Thiele's Princess Charlotte Pudding

Ingredients
1 pint milk
½ cup granulated sugar
1 tablespoon cornstarch
2 eggs
½ ounce granulated gelatin or ½ small envelope Knox Gelatine
2 ounces water
½ pint whipping cream
granulated sugar to taste
vanilla to taste
6–8 medium sized roasted almonds
Tart fruit juice (such as raspberry, strawberry or loganberry)

Directions
In a double boiler, combine milk, sugar, cornstarch and eggs. Stir this cream while cooking until it becomes a very smooth custard cream, and then let it cool to about 60 degrees Fahrenheit. Dissolve the gelatin in water. Heat it a little in order to thoroughly dissolve. Stir the gelatin into the custard cream until it begins to set. Beat the whipping cream until it becomes firm; sweeten it according to your taste. Add a little vanilla flavoring. Chop roasted almonds and gently fold into the cooked custard, along with the whipped cream. Fill six individual molds or a 1-quart mold and let the pudding stand in a cool place for 4 to 5 hours. Serve by pouring a tart fruit juice over it.

• • • •

THE GEORGIAN ROOM, 1933–2005

One of the best-kept secrets in Portland—the elegant Georgian Room—was located on the tenth floor of the Meier & Frank department store. One of the earliest photos of the Georgian Room was taken in 1933 soon after the Meier & Frank flagship store underwent an extensive remodel, so we know that the Georgian Room was at least seventy-two years old when it finally closed in 2005.

The dining room at the Georgian Room, with piano. *Courtesy of photographer Scott Allen Tice.*

The current flagship Meier & Frank building, purchased by the May Department Stores Company in the 1960s, began with the demolition of the original 1898 building, located at 136 Front Street. The building—a glazed terra-cotta fifteen-story structure—was constructed in stages. It began in 1909, with expansions during 1915 and 1932. From the website Portland History (pdxhistory.com), information from a story called "Meet Me Under the Clock" details the building's history: "In 1913, the five-story building built in 1898 at 5th & Morrison came down and work began on an addition to the 10-story Annex. The new building covered three-fourths of the block and it was completed in 1915. Over the next few years, the remaining quarter block at 6th & Morrison was purchased, the existing building was demolished and the Meier & Frank building, which now covered a full block, was fully completed in 1932."

In that Morrison Street Meier & Frank location, there was a soda fountain and a tea room, including a dairy lunch counter that was included in the store by 1920. The new Meier & Frank location replaced the five-story building, which was a pale buff-colored structure with terra-cotta trim. The site of the full block, bounded by Southwest Fifth and Sixth Avenues and Morrison and Alder Streets, has undergone numerous changes over the decades. Native Oregonian and technical writer Pam Falcioni shared what she learned about the customs of those early days of department store tea rooms like the Georgian Room in wonderful detail:

> *At that time many ladies would not be comfortable eating without a male escort at regular stand-alone restaurants. And restaurants would turn away unaccompanied women, so these early department stores would always have something like a tea room or even an ice cream parlor or sweet shop that offered light meals. Things didn't start to change until the 1920s when luncheonettes, coffee shops and hamburger places started popping up to replace taverns and fancier establishments that had relied heavily on alcohol sales prior to prohibition.*

The Georgian Room had a distinctive and understated elegance and sophistication that seemed to appeal to women mostly, and it experienced its heyday primarily during the 1940s and 1950s. Back in those days, the Georgian Room was well known as a place where dignified ladies lunched on Chicken à la King, simple sandwiches, crisp iceberg lettuce salads, small dishes of cottage cheese or fruit cups.

Christine Curran wrote a charming article about the Georgian Room for the *Oregon Historical Society Magazine* and recalled the appeal of the Georgian Room thusly: "It was glamorous and old fashioned at the same time and appealed to our sensibilities, both sophisticated and sheltered."

As a place where women gathered and felt safe, the demographic was older widows and mothers and daughters. The soups that were served were quite popular, such as the French onion, minestrone and its popular butternut squash soup. The soup was complemented, of course, by the salad bar, which was also one of the most thoroughly stocked salad bars in the city. The Cobb salad was one of its most popular lunch salads.

All during the decades the Georgian Room was open, there was a feeling that one was dining in an atmosphere steeped in the romantic mists of elegant American history, primarily because of the aristocratic ambiance the Georgian Room projected. With the light sea foam green walls, pretty crystal chandeliers and the thick draperies, one felt special simply being there. And with a particularly courtly wait staff, even a humble Portlander felt appreciated and respected as they enjoyed a modest lunch with hot coffee.

The Georgian Room became well known for its excellent beef liver and onions, when only a handful of places served liver and onions. Its version was unique because the liver was always sliced in exceptionally long, thin strips rather than thick slabs, and it was smothered with perfectly sautéed, tender golden brown onions.

The colorful and impressive club sandwich was popular, along with the homemade potato salad, which complemented its sandwiches perfectly. It also had its version of the Monte Cristo sandwich, which was prepared with sliced ham, turkey and Swiss cheese and put between grilled French toast, dusted generously with powdered confectioners' sugar and served with a side of fresh strawberry jam.

There was the lobster Thermidor, fish and chips, open-faced turkey sandwich with light brown gravy, the Crab Louie and its fine whipped mashed potatoes with dark brown gravy served with entrées or as a side. Other popular sandwiches included the excellent tuna, chicken and egg salad and its generous roast beef sandwich. Of course, the Georgian Room had formal teas with various finger sandwiches—the kind with the crusts carefully sliced off—such as cucumber and watercress. Some people, wanting a light lunch, had a small green salad or a Cobb salad with one of its warm sourdough rolls, served with fresh butter.

For dessert, the Georgian Room had several flavors of creamy milkshakes, berry pies and yellow and white cakes, including its rich dark chocolate cake. It had a tapioca pudding in a sundae dish with a dollop of whipped cream and a Maraschino cherry on top. And there was the popular silver dish of red peppermint ice cream. An exotic dessert treat offered at the Georgian Room was the papaya ice cream dessert, which was a hollowed-out papaya shell with vanilla ice cream puréed with the fresh papaya, poured back in the papaya shell and chilled.

When meeting for lunch at the Georgian Room, friends and family would often tell one another, "Meet me under the clock!" The clock in question was a large and imposing mechanical wonder. It rested high on the wall, on the south side of Meier & Frank's main floor near the middle of the room, with the elevators nearby. From there, eager customers would rise up to the tenth floor and enter the Georgian Room. No matter who you were when you visited the ornate and elegant Georgian Room, you were made to feel special.

FRYER'S QUALITY PIE, 1934–1992

Fryer's Quality Pie opened in 1934 and had an amazing run, staying open almost sixty years. It did a bustling business in Northwest Portland, with waitresses yelling orders to the cooks from behind the front counter area and into the cramped, humid kitchen. Quality Pie was fortunate to have a prime restaurant location at Northwest Twenty-Third and Northrup, with the brick and cinder-block building conveniently located across the street from Legacy Good Samaritan Hospital.

Quality Pie was open twenty-four hours a day—hours of operation that helped create a cult following for what Portland locals affectionately called "QP's." The restaurant became a trendy place to get together with friends and family and watch all sorts of unexpected and sometimes oddball characters interacting with one another.

After its early life, when the interior of the restaurant became somewhat run-down, it was referred to as Portland's best "greasy spoon" by its devoted fans. This included local hipsters and all sorts of characters. Sara Alexis Miller, a longtime customer, remembered "drag queens swapping makeup tips with the waitresses at 5:00 a.m." and an assortment of other colorful Portlanders and out-of-towners.

Customers included artists, registered nurses, writers, nursing students from Good Samaritan Hospital, professional musicians, businessmen and recovering alcoholics who frequented the AA hotspot meeting place

An early photo of Fryer's Quality Pie, circa 1930s. © *Thomas Robinson.*

located in a nearby restored mansion on Kearney Street. There were poets, insomniacs, soft-spoken middle-aged heroin addicts and other wandering eccentrics, all of whom called Quality Pie their second home. For people seeking shelter from the shadowy tree-laden streets of Northwest—in search of a hot cup of Joe and away from the wet city streets—Quality Pie was always there. Like a reliable uncle with a kind word and a welcoming slap on the back—a Denny's of sorts for Portland misfits.

When it came to food, Quality Pie offered more than just pie, often served à la mode. It had fries smothered in chicken or peppery country gravy; good standard cheeseburgers with the "big French fries"; hearty T-bone steaks; enormous strawberry, vanilla and chocolate milkshakes in the metal containers; an oyster stew; minestrone soup; a fruit cup with cottage cheese; an open-faced turkey sandwich covered in gravy; and roast beef dinners. It also had a large assortment of all-day breakfast dishes, maple bars, taco omelets, hot fudge sundaes and, of course, that famous banana split.

While Quality Pie was known for its pie, which was excellent, it also had a bottomless dime cup of coffee served in short yet sturdy yellow and brown Melamine cups. So while they had an endless cup of coffee, customers didn't get much coffee per cup. For many years, the coffee deal attracted a large number of homeless folks and resident "winos" looking to sober up or warm their bones from the ever-present rain and wind.

Quality Pie was known for its understanding and accepting attitude regarding the regular influx of Portland weirdos. The management seemed to compensate for this by having what many called "the meanest waitresses" in town. Quality Pie waitresses were more than willing to toss you out if you began drunkenly yelling into your cup of coffee about the misery of your life, verbally abusing your neighbor on the adjacent stool or aggressively asking people, "Ya got five dollars?!"

The restaurant was composed of a long section of comfortable booths upholstered in various shades of beige or off-white vinyl. The booths had large windows facing east, with the Good Samaritan Emergency Room entrance/exit within view across the street. Customers entered Quality Pie through consistently grimy glass doors that were always in need of Windex and paper towels. The waitresses washed the glass doors relentlessly, to no avail.

At one time, the foyer had three swinging glass doors—one facing east, the other south and another west. In that area, you could set aside your umbrella, kick the water off your boots and stamp them on the carpet. Then you walked through another glass door that led directly into the often stuffy

QP's on a typical busy day, circa 1980s. *Courtesy of Herb Swanson.*

restaurant interior with cigarette smoke drifting to the ceiling in languid lavender and gray tendrils—this before smoking in restaurants was made illegal in Portland. Amazingly, to stay in supply of cigarettes, the large cigarette machine in the foyer often had to be restocked twice in a twenty-four-hour period because it seemed that everyone smoked.

The booths were located to the right; on the left was the long, crowded counter in front of the kitchen area. There sat the Radio Cab drivers with longshoreman and the Esco Steel workers, all loading up on breakfast and coffee before work. There were several tables in the back, and to the left were the restrooms, which always smelled like cleaning fluid. The carpeting of Quality Pie, after so many years of serving Portlanders, had numerous stains dotted here and there, including cigarette burns. It was so threadbare in sections that customers could feel the concrete flooring beneath their feet. Darlene Gunderson remembered the clientele well and how colorful and fun the atmosphere could be: "Lots of loud people who mostly knew each other acting out, making out and hanging out," she said.

In the late 1950s and early 1960s, Quality Pie was as popular with high school kids as it would be in the 1970s and 1980s, when kids would crowd the counter after school, ordering slices of lemon, apple and berry pie and washing them down with big glasses of ice-cold milk. Teenagers would arrive in large groups, sometimes getting scolded by the tough Quality Pie waitresses, who took no guff and told them "Knock it off!" and "Be quiet!" or the sterner, "If you kids don't quiet down, you're gonna leave!"

Roger Kofler of Portland remembered when a buddy wouldn't take no for an answer when the staff ran out of bananas for the popular banana split: "In the early 1960s, some of my friends and I used to hang out at QP, and one of my friends liked banana splits. One night, my friend Dick Lively ordered his banana split, and the waitress smugly informed him that they were out of bananas. Across Twenty-Third, there was a little old grocery store. I think it was called Karfotia's. Dick ran out the door of QP and down to the grocery and bought a banana, came back and handed it to that waitress. You should've seen the look on her face!"

In the 1970s and 1980s, there was a pay phone in the foyer that often had a line of people waiting to use it. Quiet low-key drug deals were rampant at Quality Pie in those years, often facilitated by the pay phone, with the discreet heroin addicts trying to score a fix. Eventually, the pay phone was removed. It was for this reason that spoons had to be restocked monthly because they routinely went missing, at quite a cost to the restaurant. Former owner Larry Cervarich remembered the dilemma well: "It didn't take long to figure out why we were missing so many teaspoons! Until we checked the bathrooms! It was the most expensive item to continually replace each month." Cervarich also remembered the general challenge of running Quality Pie: "It was the worst headache of my life. A zoo after hours. I definitely learned from it. Never again. We did have the best pies in the city. Try purchasing a whole pie today for $3.29. And people complained of the price!"

Darlene Olesko also remembered the QP vibe perfectly: "Go-go girls and strippers from Sonny's Lounge and other bars, cops on coffee breaks, great hamburgers and wonderful Coconut Cream Pie, working girls, night people."

John Lawrence Kennedy, a transplant from Texas and longtime Oregon resident, recalled working as a dishwasher at Quality Pie in the late 1980s. Kennedy remembered that the waitresses were indeed short on patience:

The waitresses had to deal with a lot of riffraff who would come in drunk late at night. One night, after midnight, an old wino came in and sat in the middle of the counter, across from the kitchen. He was stinking drunk but said he was hungry and ordered a big stack of pancakes with hot coffee. After eating all the pancakes with a lot of butter and syrup and washing them down with lots of hot coffee and within only a minute or two of finishing the whole stack, the guy projectile vomited the entire mess across the counter onto the other side. It landed on the coffee maker and inside the coffee urn. It was a huge foul mess. I know because I had to clean it up. Then he stumbled out with the waitresses yelling at him and without paying the tab, but we didn't care. We just wanted him gone.

One devoted customer of QP was writer and poet Lisa Flowers, who lived in Portland in the 1990s. She recalled the scene at Quality Pie and how fun, chaotic and eclectic it could be, especially after hours:

During the late 1980s to 1991, when I was a delinquent teen sporting jet-black hair, Ben Ney "Clown White" makeup as foundation, and Artmatic "Black Orchid" lipstick (purchased for 99 cents at Newberry's downtown), I spent my nights at the City Nightclub and many evenings ended at QP's. The atmosphere was like a Tom Waits song, crossed with a bit of the diner scenes from Martin Scorsese's film Taxi Driver—*a pitch-perfect counterculture after-hours fever dream. If we were stoned and had the munchies, the table ended up looking like a group of two-year-olds in high chairs had just left. The greatest drag queens in the world would be at QP's, coked to the gills, and sometimes lines were snorted right there at the table. I had been told of the surliness of the waitresses, and they lived up to the hype—fabulous, like fuming bulls ready to charge, tense, cinematic. But good sorts who had just seen too much. We would sit there for hours drinking coffee and rarely tipping because we were young and dumb. But in hindsight, it was the very last part of a priceless era of Americana in Portland.*

Portland writer and English professor Steffen Silvis remembered his time at Quality Pie and the inclusive atmosphere where people from all walks of life were happy to sit and talk and laugh about life: "One night at the counter I saw a couple of drag queens sitting next to cops and dock workers. It was probably about 3:00 a.m. When I decided that I wanted to really be a writer, I went to QP, sat at the counter at around 11:00 p.m. and just wrote all through the night until about 5:00 a.m., fueled on coffee and pie."

Eventually, Quality Pie shuttered in 1992. The building was in terrible condition and had leaks due to the crumbling walls and ceiling, and the restaurant needed a complete overhaul. Neighbors had long complained about the restaurant being open to the wee hours of the night. The folks from the nearby Alcoholics Anonymous (people known to go to the Night Owls Meeting) were often loud, and occasionally there would be a fight in the parking lot. People sleeping in nearby houses grew tired of the disturbances, having to call the police to break up fights and send people on their way.

There was a lot of grumbling from the Portland community when it was announced that QP's would close because it was such a beloved landmark. However, because it became such a legend, there is a Seattle company, Printing and Graphic Design, that prints charming Quality Pie T-shirts for the modest sum of twenty-five dollars. The simple white shirts come in all sizes and have the words "Quality Pie, Portland Oregon" emblazoned over the front in black lettering. For the hardcore Quality Pie fan who still misses the old days, when they could watch their favorite QP waitress yell at a customer, sigh in disgust or roll their eyes at an unusual food order request, which they might then refuse with aplomb and casual grace.

Chapter 3

More Comfort Food

THE CHOCOLATE LOUNGE/ORANGE SLICE, 1937–1986

The Chocolate Lounge was located on the mezzanine floor directly next to the book department in the Lipman Wolfe & Company department store. It was located in the heart of downtown Portland and was a lunchroom frequented mostly by women—widows, wives or mothers who often went to afternoon lunches minus their children for a break.

Adolphe Wolf, who was from Germany, came to America and, together with his uncle, Solomon Lipman, opened up Lipman Wolfe & Company and became successful merchants. The Lipman & Wolfe department store, where the Chocolate Lounge was ensconced, was its flagship location and designed by architects Doyle & Patterson. It was also known in professional circles for establishing several firsts in retail history.

In an online article from the website Portland History, it is revealed that Lipman & Wolfe was the first department store in the nation to introduce elevators to take customers between floors so they wouldn't have to trudge up and down cold, drafty stairwells: "Wolfe set up shop in a building at Washington and First streets where Portland's first store elevator transported patrons vertically. His customers marveled at being able to move among the other floors without using stairs. Following the lead of fellow merchant Henry Corbett, Lipman & Wolfe Company closed the store on Sundays."

The store was the first to mark set prices on merchandise, which eliminated the age-old custom of haggling between the seller and buyer, a tradition

LOST RESTAURANTS OF PORTLAND, OREGON

going back to the turn of the century: "Lipman & Wolfe also started the practice of making change down to the penny, instead of down to the last nickel, as was the custom of the day. This forced the Ladd & Tilton Bank to telegraph for supplies of copper pennies, which prior to this time were not readily available. Until the coppers arrived, Lipman Wolfe & Co. made change with postage stamps."

When the Chocolate Lounge first opened in 1937, part of its immense appeal was its mezzanine setting, which had an impressive view of the store. The restaurant consisted of a long, narrow space with an unhindered, nearly perfect view of the first floor below. The dining area was protected only by a decorative, waist-high ornamental grille painted thickly with glossy white enamel paint. At

The Chocolate Lounge at Lipman, Wolfe & Co. It was a place to be seen in your best ensemble. *Alfred Monner / 1951*

Ladies lunching, 1951. *Courtesy of photographer Scott Allen Tice.*

the far north end of the restaurant, the wall was covered in glittering mirrors that were cleaned and polished often. The squares of mirror, secured to the wall, gave the space a feeling of being larger than it really was and added illumination.

If you were waiting for a girlfriend and spied her walking in the southeast doors, or she spied you sitting in the restaurant above, you could discreetly wave and she knew exactly where you were. Sitting above the bustling commotion gave patrons a feeling that they were part of something, even if they ate their lunch alone. The occasional teenage shoplifter being escorted out was something patrons might also see occurring on the main level, particularly during the 1980s. They might also see married couples haggling over the price of a fine pair of Italian leather gloves or a lady's brimmed hat or a bottle of expensive perfume. Perfume at Lipman & Wolfe was exceptional and included classics like Joy, Shalimar, Chanel N°5, Mitsouko and White Shoulders. The perfume counter was large and included exotic perfumes such as Etiquette Noire by Lancôme, Egyptian Bouquet and the strangely named Caucasian Allure, both sold by perfumer Prince Alex N. Gagarin.

The Chocolate Lounge was popular because of a particular carnival element. Observing shoppers while you enjoyed lunch, with browsing

74

customers blissfully unaware of any watchful eyes, was a part of that appeal. Booths and tables sat on either side of the long aisle. In front of the kitchen area to the far right was a long counter with several stools. There were painted murals with intricate cocoa beans growing and being harvested.

Food was prepared in the kitchen behind the counter, where the cooks sweated and jockeyed for adequate room in the cramped space. There were standard favorites such as cheeseburgers and club sandwiches, as well as many fine desserts. Because of its good standard fare—sandwiches, pasta and hearty salads along with the various sweet treats—the Chocolate Lounge was the perfect place to have lunch and people watch.

True to the name, the Chocolate Lounge also featured numerous chocolate desserts. This included devil's food cake, brownies, rich chocolate pudding and chocolate ice cream, along with chocolate soda drinks and a frothy concoction they called the Tiger Tigers. In the same Portland History article, the Tiger Tigers is described: "John Slocum, who worked for three summers in the Chocolate Lounge in the late 1950s, recalled making 'Tiger Tigers' (orange ice cream with chocolate swirl syrup in a parfait glass) and 'Idiot's Delight,' several scoops of ice cream of all flavors topped with a sample of all the toppings, including strawberries, chocolate syrup, marshmallows and nuts, in a large bowl."

Lipman & Wolfe, like other family-owned department stores, had the advantage of family loyalty behind its successful operation. But many department stores would end up being purchased by large chains, and Lipman & Wolfe was no different, as the website Portland History noted: "The Lipman's-Roberts Bros. stores were merged with the Dayton Corp. of Minneapolis in 1968 in a stock transaction valued at $33.3 million. Then, in 1979, the Marshall Field Company of Chicago bought all six Lipman's Stores and turned them into Frederick & Nelson stores and the Chocolate Lounge was renamed The Orange Slice."

After the surprising switch, the décor changed from hues of chocolate brown and bright white to the citrusy '70s colors of bright orange and various shades of yellow. When the transition between Lipman's and Frederick & Nelson occurred, Steffen Silvis, a young student and longtime Portland resident, was hired for the temporary work of helping to dismantle the store: "As a high school freshman, my best friend's uncle was hired to remove all of the old Lipman's cash registers and anything bearing the Lipman's name from inside the department store to make room for the Frederick and Nelson's stuff, and he hired us to help. Those old registers, which had been there since the Lipman Wolfe days, weighed a ton. It was sad seeing Lipman's stripped bare."

After the name change, most of the wait staff and the manager remained employed, carrying on the traditions of the original menu and creating a few new options, but some people had a hard time accepting the name change and rebelled. Brian Thompson, who began working at Lipman's in June 1972, recalled, "The restaurant on the mezzanine had recently been renamed the 'Orange Slice' and many regulars still called it the Chocolate Lounge. The manager was a friendly woman named Audrey Snider, and many of the employees and regulars called her Miss Audrey, even though she was married."

After Frederick & Nelson bought out the store, the renamed Orange Slice remained popular. People still ate their lunch, drank coffee or rich hot chocolate and lingered so they could watch the first-floor activities at the perfume, cosmetics, hosiery, hat and glove counters, as they always had. However, with the buyout customers were introduced to the delicious and creamy Frango chocolates made famous by the Frederick & Nelson stores. The chocolates were sold in cylindrical white cardboard boxes with decorative gold fringe. With each individual soft mint chocolate wrapped separately, the boxes were kept in a refrigerated glass case near the cash register. The naming of the candy was an interesting amalgamation of more than one name, as Portland History described: "You can't talk about Frederick & Nelson without mentioning Frango's melt-in-your-mouth chocolates. The name probably originated from FRederick And Nelson Company, or FRANCO. When the revolution occurred in Spain, the company did *not* want an association with the dictator and so FRANCO became FRANGO."

After seven years as Frederick & Nelson, the store closed suddenly one day in 1986 and made the local news for the abrupt and unprofessional manner in which the store went out of business. The Chocolate Lounge/Orange Slice was no more. Portlander Alison Chapman remembered the day well, as employees briskly walked up to the store to begin their working day and found all the doors locked and no explanation other than a scribbled note taped to the door stating that the store had gone out of business. Employees were devastated, according to Alice: "I was working at the Washington Square Frederick & Nelson when they closed the downtown store. It was a complete shock. Many of the downtown staff spent the day commiserating at the Virginia Café, where a few of us from Washington Square joined them at happy hour. By then, it had evolved to a crazy party vibe, but it was devastating to those folks who lost their jobs. Many had worked decades at Lipman & Wolfe and then later Frederick & Nelson."

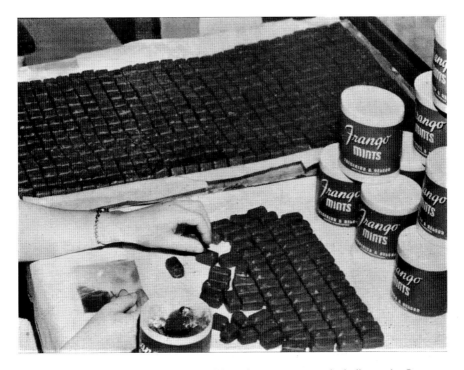

Frango mints were sold in all Frederick & Nelson department stores, including at the Orange Slice. *Courtesy of author Ann Wendell, from her book* Frederick & Nelson *(The History Press).*

After almost fifty years, the Chocolate Lounge/Orange Slice was suddenly gone and, with it, a million memories of Portlanders enjoying the heyday of department store luxury and style. For the next several months, after the closure, Portlanders and former employees were invited to begin the melancholy process of buying what remained of the furniture and other odd miscellaneous items. This took quite a while to accomplish and included numerous fine glass perfume and cosmetic counters, which were quite elaborate and heavy, and even some valuable framed prints that had been hanging in the store for decades.

Portlanders were extremely disappointed at the closure and the loss of the Christmas traditions both stores had set into motion, particularly regarding the Cinnamon Bear. Those holiday traditions had become part of Portland families' routines and holiday customs for decades.

We now live in a time when department stores are vanishing with lightning speed, particularly since the advent of online purchasing. These changes signal the end of women meeting for lunch or traditional teas, dressed in elaborate hats and gloves. In its long existence, both restaurants created countless happy memories for Portlanders. A special era in Portland ended when the Chocolate Lounge/Orange Slice abruptly shuttered with the sudden and unexpected closure of the Frederick & Nelson department store.

WADDLE'S COFFEE SHOP, 1938–2004

Waddle's Coffee Shop was founded by Gene and Natha Waddle. They opened their flagship location at Jantzen Beach the day before World War II ended in early September 1945. The building was designed by Portland's award-winning "famed architect" Pietro Belluschi. He also designed the Portland Art Museum from 1931 to 1932 and the Equitable Building, along with the Juilliard School and Lincoln Center in New York.

Although it is not listed as one of Belluschi's significant buildings, the Waddle's structure was perfect for what it was: a simple coffee shop. Belluschi produced an attractive restaurant building with a long carport area where people could park and be served out of the famous inclement weather typical of Portland.

The interior was particularly attractive, as the *Willamette Week* described, with "latticed wood stretching along its outer ceiling and a long counter wrapped around the kitchen," which Belluschi had placed on a raised pedestal to draw attention to its "magnitude." The interior of the restaurant was elegant in an understated, unassuming fashion yet was spacious enough to promote easy customer and wait staff traffic within the cheerfully modern space.

Belluschi was the same architect who designed what has been called "the world's first modern office building," located in Portland. This was known as the Equitable Building, which opened in 1948, now known as the Commonwealth Building. The structure had an unusual aluminum-glass exterior and became known for its "simple, spare, elegant" design. Belluschi designed numerous churches, including the Central Lutheran Church on Northeast Hancock Street.

Waddle's history began earlier than 1945, though, when the restaurant advertised its location as "opposite Jantzen Beach" and a "ducky place to eat" with "fine food since 1938." In its heyday, the restaurant had three prime locations, boasting in local advertisements that its restaurants were "modern," with the flagship location at Jantzen Beach Park, just south of the Columbia River. The second location was at 99E at Southeast Holgate, four

Exterior photo of Waddle's Coffee Shop. © *Thomas Robinson.*

Parking lot of Waddle's with the long carport. © *Thomas Robinson.*

miles south of the downtown business section in the city. The third location was described as a "self-service buffet" and was located at 929 Southwest Washington, in the Pittock Block.

For anyone crossing the Columbia River between Oregon and Washington, none could miss the landmark red sign visible from the freeway's northbound lanes. The sign had a large clock, with clock hands designed to look like a knife and fork and the words "Eat Now at Waddle's" prominently displayed, which served to remind everyone that it was indeed time to eat. There was a time, though, when Waddle's had a wooden sign that read, "We Cater Only to the White Trade," which was near the carport area. That sign was later removed after a remodel several years later and after numerous people from both Oregon and Washington objected to the blatant and offensive racism of the sign.

After Gene and Natha Waddle opened up their flagship location, Waddle's became known as a family dining destination and the place to go for delicious comfort food. When the Jantzen Beach location first opened, it was known as Waddle's Coffee Shop and became so popular that sometimes there were lines of hungry families waiting to get inside almost a block long.

Waddle's specialty was comfort food, including its hearty omelets and cottage fried potatoes, which could be covered with a generous helping of country gravy. One of its popular sandwiches was called the Double Duck Hamburger, which had two hamburger patties and a special sauce, including a rarebit sauce that was legendary. Waddle's had pies, cakes, blackberry cobbler, a popular chicken basket, French toast and corned beef hash. Another popular dish was called the Mount Hood, which comprised baked, open-faced hamburger buns slathered with garlic butter and a hamburger patty on each bun slice, topped with savory chili. For "snow," the chili was topped with bits of fresh chopped onion.

After sixty years of great meals and excellent service, along with the death of Gene Waddle, who was the original owner, the restaurant was shuttered. There was something of a dispute about the owner of the building continually raising the rent. Russell Waddle, Gene Waddle's son, had strongly objected to the harsh increase. The younger Waddle felt that the increase in rent was not warranted, and so the lease was not renewed and the restaurant shuttered in 2004. The family considered relocating down the street in the same area, but the cost would have been exorbitant, so they chose to close permanently instead.

This beloved Portland culinary destination was then replaced by a chain restaurant: Hooter's. Hooter's decided to keep the "Eat Now at Waddle's"

Exterior view of the building, designed by Pietro Belluschi. © *Thomas Robinson.*

sign but altered it to read "Eat Now at Hooter's." And the little Waddle's duckling wearing his Waddle's bib was replaced by the Hooter's Owl. Many Portlanders were outraged at the new sign and vowed never to eat there, as it could never be the same as when the restaurant was the one and only Waddle's, famous for its creative and delicious comfort food and homey, welcoming atmosphere.

DUPAY'S DRIVE-IN RESTAURANT, 1954–1962

DuPay's Drive-In Restaurant became popular in Portland during the prosperity of the 1950s. It was during the heyday of the drive-in restaurant, when pretty carhops dressed in hoop skirts were all the rage as they occupied the collective consciousness of American popular culture.

DuPay's was owned and operated by S.M. DuPay and his wife, Clara, both originally from Montana, with help from their hardworking teenage son Don DuPay, who worked as the fountain manager—a soda jerk, dishwasher and fry cook all in one. Don DuPay's younger twin sisters, Joanne and Jeanne DuPay, were also employed at the restaurant, where they worked hard as cashiers and hostesses and bused tables.

The catchy slogan "It pays to eat at DuPay's!" was included on menus, business cards and newspaper advertisements, which helped spread the word about the trendy restaurant. It was a large operation, located at 4534 Southeast McLoughlin Boulevard (presently La Carreta Mexican Restaurant) and was formerly another location for Waddle's, owned by Gene Waddle. Waddle remained friendly with the DuPay family after selling them his business, at which point the DuPays opened their drive-in, replete with carhop waitresses, elaborate Sunday dinners and a full-service bar upstairs on the second floor.

In its most productive years, DuPay's had five cooks, six carhop waitresses, more than twenty waitresses, two bartenders, two soda jerks and two janitors. One of the carhop waitresses became something of a legend in her own right and had a bevy of admirers from the Portland Police Bureau, among other interested males who frequented the drive-in. Miss Barbara Clemo was a local Portland girl, and at five-foot-four, with dyed black hair and bright-red lipstick, she personified 1950s cuteness and feminine appeal. With a slender build and a famously large bust, Miss Clemo was never short of fans. According to Don DuPay, who remembered Miss Clemo well, she was "the reason the cops came around."

Don DuPay also remembered the two Koffey brothers, Don and Clay, who worked for the Portland Police Bureau as respected street cops: "The Koffey brothers came for coffee every day, and it became kind of a joke because of their name. 'The Koffey brothers are coming to get coffee!' I admired them because they were friendly and talked to me. They would invite me to sit in their car and listen to the radio as it crackled, and they always answered my questions about law enforcement. They seemed in charge, confident and decent men. I looked up to them. In the end, the

FEATURING
CHICKEN ☆ STEAK ☆ LITTLE THIN PANCAKES

DUPAY'S RESTAURANT

COCKTAIL LOUNGES   PARTY ROOMS

Heresto Pands Pen Dasoci Alhou Rinhar Mles Smirt Hand Funl
Etfri Ends Hipre Ign Bejus Tand Kindan Devils Peak Of No Ne.

SHERLEY & CLARA DuPAY   4534 S.E. McLOUGHLIN
BELMONT 4-2525   PORTLAND 2, OREGON

Top: The DuPay family portrait, circa 1952: S.M. DuPay, Clara DuPay and their children, Don, Jeanne and Joanne DuPay. *Courtesy of photographer Scott Allen Tice, obtained by Theresa Griffin Kennedy.*

Bottom: A DuPay business card, circa 1950s. *Courtesy of Theresa Griffin Kennedy.*

Koffey brothers were the reason I became a police officer with the Portland Police Bureau."

DuPay's Drive-In had a main dining area, with windows facing north and west, with room enough to seat more than sixty people. There was an even larger banquet hall upstairs on the second level with a fully stocked bar. The upstairs area was often used for birthdays, anniversaries, wedding receptions, baby shower celebrations and high school proms. Being so large—it had room for more than two hundred diners—it served various clubs, such as the Rotary Club and the Portland Toastmasters International.

For the upstairs banquet hall, food was prepared in the main kitchen and delivered via a small electric elevator called a dumbwaiter. On a large plastic tray, the cooks would crowd four to six plates of steaming hot food, which was then delivered via the dumbwaiter to the hungry patrons waiting above. This simplified delivery and resulted in fewer broken dishes from accidents. There was a full-service fountain area in the kitchen where soda jerks served up milkshakes in flavors like strawberry, chocolate, banana and peanut butter. There were root beer floats and ice cream sodas in vanilla, chocolate and strawberry. It had traditional banana splits and chocolate, strawberry, butterscotch and hot fudge sundaes. Soft drinks included the famous Green River soda and any number of other sweet drinks, including the original cherry and chocolate Coke drinks that had to be hand-mixed, along with fresh-squeezed orange juice, lemonade, orangeade, limeade and its Orange Freeze drink.

Business at DuPay's was often so hectic that S.M. and Clara decided to carry on Gene Waddle's tradition of using a special code for the soda fountain orders to expedite service during afternoon and evening rushes. This was done by using a certain terminology. For example, a "shake" was always vanilla. But if a customer wanted a chocolate shake or a strawberry shake, the waitress would ask for a "chocolate shake" or "strawberry shake." A sundae was always called an "on," with the waitress saying, "I need an on!" because the syrup went *on* the top, and for that reason it was understood to be a vanilla sundae with chocolate syrup.

If a waitress needed to order a soda float, like a root beer float, she would say, "I need an in!" which was always understood to be a float with vanilla ice cream *in* the soda. If the waitress needed a different kind of soda float, she would say, "I need a chocolate in!" or "I need a strawberry in!" If a customer wanted a simple Coke, the waitress would say, "I need a shot!" If the customer wanted a flavored Coke, the waitress either said, "I need a chocolate shot!" or "I need a cherry shot!" If a customer wanted both a cherry and a chocolate Coke, the waitress would say, "Shoot a pair left and right!" This was done because the cherry syrup pump and the chocolate syrup pump were located next to each other on the soda fountain. Using this odd terminology, business was conducted much quicker.

Food items at DuPay's included its popular hamburgers, which were actually listed as "steer burgers" and made from fresh-ground chuck. The steer burgers were prepared with all the fixings, if that was what the customer wanted. Steer burgers could be ordered with a rarebit sauce, which was made from cheese and beer. The rarebit recipe was shared with the DuPay family by Gene Waddle and remained a constant favorite appreciated and shared by more than one Portland restaurant.

The sauce required one can of beer to prepare. One of the cooks at the time, Frank, would often requisition three cans of beer from the upstairs bar, explaining that he had to make some rarebit sauce. After walking upstairs for the beer, Jack would then walk back downstairs to the kitchen and proceed to drink two of the beers, using only one can for the rarebit sauce. This happened regularly according to Don DuPay, who sometimes chuckled to himself while watching Jack cheerfully break the rules. DuPay explained that times were different then: "It would get hot in that kitchen, and because the cooks were king at DuPay's, they got away with a lot."

DuPay's was a family restaurant with a popular Sunday dinner, which included prime rib, turkey and steak dinners. There was a special Easter Sunday dinner that included a roast leg of spring lamb with dressing and roast young turkey with dressing and cranberry sauce. DuPay's also prepared a baked Virginia ham with orange sauce, fried spring chicken, "one half unjointed," and a Hawaiian ham steak with a grilled pineapple ring. For its Easter Sunday menu, DuPay's featured baked Swiss steak with sauce, grilled halibut steak, grilled red king salmon and fried Louisiana jumbo shrimp with red sauce. Most meals were served with a baked potato, or French fried potatoes, and a hot roll with fresh butter. Desserts included lime and orange sherbet, fresh fruit cobbler, custard pudding with whipped cream and a blackberry sundae made from "wild picked" blackberries.

For many years, DuPay's drinks were only a dime. The hot drinks included hot coffee, Sanka coffee, Postum, hot chocolate and tea. Cold drinks included soda, iced tea, milk and, of course, the ever-popular fresh buttermilk that was routinely requested.

To supplement DuPay's restaurant with seafood, Clara DuPay, an avid fisherwoman, would take time off to go salmon or trout fishing at Garibaldi Bay on the Oregon coast. Sometimes Clara would disregard that inconvenient rule that you needed a license to fish. She had grown up in rural Dupuyer, Montana, on a family farm and had lived off the land for as long as she could remember. Clara didn't feel it was necessary to pay the state to fish, particularly if it was only to catch a small batch for subsistence or to supplement their restaurant. On one such occasion in 1952, Clara "dragged" sixteen-year-old Don to fish with her and, after several hours of fishing, was cited by a game warden for not having a license. Don recalled, "I was mad she would go fishing without a license. I told her, 'I told you so! I told you so!' I hated fishing because it was so smelly and disgusting, and on the day that she got the ticket, I was mad because it was also embarrassing."

DuPay's had shrimp Louis and Dungeness crab Louis and excellent fresh-caught salmon when seafood was in season. It had a generous "Combination Sea Food Plate" for a whopping $1.65. It included crab legs, prawns, scallops, halibut, DuPay's homemade special coleslaw ("served with tangy sour cream dressing") and French fried potatoes. It also served its popular large Louisiana prawns, deep-sea eastern scallops and grilled Alaska halibut steak.

Sandwiches at DuPay's included cold turkey, cold roast beef and an open-faced turkey sandwich with giblet gravy, served with potatoes and cranberry sauce. Other sandwiches included corned beef, egg salad, tuna salad and its popular BLTs. DuPay's popular soups were prepared exclusively by S.M. DuPay, who had a knack for making homemade soup using old recipes he brought to Portland from his family in Bozeman, Montana. The soups included clam chowder, split pea, chicken noodle and a creamy tomato bisque soup that was popular because of the hearty chunks of fresh tomato. Desserts included ice cream, cheesecake and cherry, pumpkin and lemon meringue pies, which were made fresh every day in the restaurant by Clara DuPay.

DuPay's proudly served Boyd's Coffee, which was available with all meals and sold to the family by Bill Roylance, who would become longtime friends with S.M., Clara and Don. Roylance would ultimately open up a restaurant of his own and call it the River Queen, but back in the days of DuPay's Drive-In, Roylance was simply a traveling coffee salesman with big dreams of the restaurant business. Once a month, Roylance came by DuPay's with the monthly coffee order, and after the formalities of business were concluded, Roylance would sit and commiserate with S.M. and Clara for an hour or two. During the monthly visits, Roylance would share his dream of opening his own restaurant, asking questions about the business, with Don listening nearby.

OAK PIT

6878 N. Lombard   AVenue 6-0831

The Oak Pit restaurant, circa 1960s. *Courtesy of Scott Allen Tice.*

There was another aspect of DuPay's that made it unique. For customers who wanted to be discreet about their drinking habits, or who they might be spending time with, there was a private staircase leading up to the second-floor bar, which was accessible from the outside. The doorway leading up the dimly lit stairs was always unlocked during business hours, and customers regularly used the second outside entrance to the bar because it was so private. This made hookups and unobtrusive drinking possible for those with secrets to guard.

Right about the time S.M. and Clara DuPay's son, Don, began his career as a Portland police officer in 1961, the DuPays were approaching middle age, and the work and responsibility of maintaining and operating such a large restaurant became too difficult. As their oldest child had more interest in law enforcement than in taking over the restaurant, DuPay's Drive-In was shuttered with very little fanfare or media notice.

A few months later, the DuPays took over a small restaurant that had been in business for several years already called the Oak Pit Barbecue. Their new place kept them busy but not overwhelmed. The Oak Pit was located in St. John's on Lombard and Ida and was a popular hangout for the teenage students at Roosevelt High School. The Oak Pit was as popular as DuPay's Drive-In had been and continued well into the late 1960s.

THE HOLLYWOOD BURGER BAR, 1954–2015

One small restaurant that became a favorite of Portlanders was the Hollywood Burger Bar on Forty-Second and Northeast Sandy Boulevard in the heart of the Hollywood District. Since 1954, the modest building often housed some form of restaurant dedicated to the grilling and serving of simple burgers. The odd-looking building had a long counter with seats for fifteen people and three tables with space for twelve more customers. Orders were taken at the counter, and on a busy day, the small space could get cramped and stuffy with hungry patrons while to-go orders or sit-down orders were being prepared.

The building began as a trolley stop and tollbooth around 1922 and was used in that capacity as a ticket office and lobby for streetcar lines that intersected at Sandy and Forty-Second Avenue. Later, it became Allyn's Cleaners from 1930 to 1937. After that, it became the Wee Maid Ice Cream shop from 1937 to 1954, at which time the small structure finally transformed into a restaurant, going through several owners during its long life as a burger joint.

Longtime owner Inka Elliott, with her late husband, Craig, had a loyal customer base. They took over the Hollywood Burger Bar in 1989, finally selling it in October 2013 after almost twenty-five years in operation. Their menu was standard for a burger restaurant, with a selection of delicious burgers, sandwiches and breakfast options served all day. The Special Burger was simply the Original Burger but with ham, a fried egg and melted cheese. There was the chili burger, the bacon cheeseburger and the notoriously rich and delicious Hollywood Ultimate Double Burger, which consisted of two

Advertising graphic for the Hollywood Burger Bar. *Courtesy of photographer Scott Allen Tice.*

Street view of the Hollywood Burger Bar. *Courtesy of photographer Scott Allen Tice.*

Exterior view of the Hollywood Burger Bar. *Courtesy of photographer Scott Allen Tice.*

ground beef patties with bacon, Swiss and cheddar cheese and any number of other ingredients to complete it.

Geoff Kleinman, a former Portlander who wrote restaurant reviews online, remembered the Hollywood Burger Bar and the perfect burgers it served in this excellent 2010 review:

Original Burger—1/3 pound ground beef patty on a sesame seed bun with 1000 Island, mayo, lettuce, tomato, pickle & onion for $5.75. I added cheese for $0.50 and had an iced tea for $1.50. My order total was $7.75. The burger took a good 10–15 minutes to come up. My iced tea came up pretty quick and it was amazingly strong. I liked the way my burger came up, presented on a platter with the fries—it felt like a Burger 101 diagram. I piled all the fixings on and took my first bite. WOW! There is a reason why this burger is presented like a Burger 101 diagram: it is a perfect example of how a classic hamburger works, with the mayo on the bottom and the thousand island on the top with the burger and toppings encased in creamy goodness. The crispness of the lettuce and richness of the tomato balance perfectly with the sharpness of the onion and the savory sour pickle. The sesame seed bun is cooked to absolute crispy perfection and encases it all in a sweet and crunchy pocket. And then there's the burger, cooked medium-well, a perfect union between the crispy char on the outside and the juicy meat on the inside. Every element of this burger comes together perfectly. The title of "best burger in Portland" is something that can be debated ad infinitum, so it's enough to simply say that Hollywood Burger Bar's Original Burger is one superb, classic hamburger.

A visual of the perfect hamburger from the Hollywood Burger Bar. *Courtesy of photographer of Scott Allen Tice.*

Various awards from burger contests. *Courtesy of photographer Scott Allen Tice.*

The Hollywood Burger Bar was so beloved that it was entered into several "Best Burger" contests. In 2005, it was listed as having one of the city's best burgers by the AOL CityGuide, as well as by the Cascade Blues Association.

There were other things on the menu besides burgers, fries and onion rings. There was the lunch menu with the country fried steak with gravy; soup and salad; the chef salad; and a Greek gyro consisting of seasoned strips of meat, with onion, tomato, lettuce and tzatziki sauce wrapped nicely in pita bread. There was the patty melt, a third-pound ground beef patty, with Swiss cheese and grilled onion on grilled rye bread. It had a standard hot dog on a bun, served with a variety of mustards, cheese and chili. It served the Club House Special and the teriyaki chicken sandwich. The chicken cordon bleu sandwich was particularly tasty and popular. It consisted of a breaded chicken patty on a hoagie bun with thin-sliced ham, Swiss cheese and honey mustard. It also served a fish sandwich and a chicken patty melt sandwich.

Breakfast dishes were numerous and included hash browns, eggs, toast, bacon, sausage or thick-sliced ham, as well as diced ham with scrambled eggs. It had a veggie omelet, chili cheese omelet and a Denver omelet, along with waffles, pancakes, biscuits and gravy and the fully loaded breakfast burritos. The Hollywood Burger Bar was often the winner of the Best

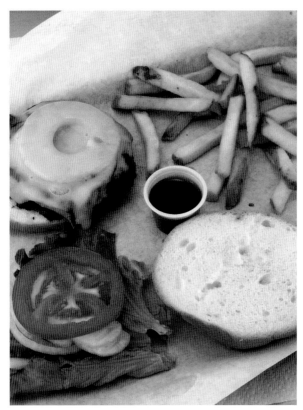

Left: Another great-looking sandwich. *Courtesy of photographer Scott Allen Tice.*

Below: A wonderful photo of the intersection near the Hollywood Burger Bar, circa 1970s. *Courtesy of photographer Scott Allen Tice.*

Opposite: A perfect-looking banana split. *Courtesy of photographer Scott Allen Tice.*

Burger in Portland contest, which occurred several times and was publicized all through Portland, with local media coming by for interviews.

In 2003, Portland artist Jonie DeRouchie recommended the Hollywood Burger Bar to several of her friends who were looking for the perfect filming location:

> *I was directing a short film called* Remote Control *that I'd co-written with my partner, Rick Emerson, who was a local talk radio personality in Portland for many years. Rick was also starring in the film and several other local actors. We had made arrangements to shoot our diner scene at Leo's Smoke-Free Coffee Shop downtown, but when we showed up on the afternoon we were to film (actors in costume and gear in hand), the manager pulled the plug on the agreement. Not to be daunted, our location guy, Aaron Duran, scrambled to find another location and got Hollywood Burger Bar to agree. We showed up at closing, the manager handed over the keys, told us to lock up and left. We shot until the sun came up. Being a newbie, I hadn't anticipated the noise restaurant equipment makes. Though we desperately wanted to unplug everything, we wanted to be respectful to the incredibly kind people who allowed a bunch of strangers to invade their restaurant with nothing to offer in return. Consequently, the film is full of troublesome humming noises and the sounds of refrigerators running. Nevertheless, shooting there was a blast, and it turned out to be the perfect spot for our folksy diner location.*

After sixty-one years, the Hollywood Burger Bar was shuttered in 2013, eventually making room for Reo's Ribs, which was owned and operated by the late Reo Varnado, who was often seen at Portland blues shows and was the uncle to legendary rapper Snoop Dogg. Varnado's ribs were a Snoop Dogg favorite—he enjoyed them so much he would arrange large orders of his uncle's ribs to be delivered to him even while he was on the road and on tour.

At the time of the closure of the Hollywood Burger Bar, the oddly whimsical ninety-three-year-old building had gained landmark status, officially becoming a Portland icon of sorts. After the Hollywood Burger Bar closed, many Portlanders became concerned that developers would try to buy up the property and demolish the small building,

but that has not happened. The main reason is because the area is so small and problematic that nothing of any size could be developed there. As a result, the building remains intact today, due in large part to being an undesirable spot for developers. It may not be the Hollywood Burger Bar anymore, but the quaint little building is still a restaurant and still serving hungry residents. After the beloved Reo Varnado passed away in January 2022, the restaurant was taken over by family and friends and is still delighting Portland residents with delicious Reo's ribs and other delectable barbecue.

Chapter 4
Entertainment, Soul Food and Racism

SAMBO'S RESTAURANT, 1957–1981

The first Sambo's restaurant opened on June 17, 1957, at 216 West Cabrillo Boulevard in Santa Barbara, California. At its height, there would be more than one thousand Sambo's Restaurants throughout the country, including several in the state of Oregon. Despite the chain eventually filing for bankruptcy and shuttering all its locations, the first Sambo's in Santa Barbara is still open today, run by Chad Stevens, the original owner's grandson.

However, on July 9, 2020, following the horrific homicide of George Floyd in Minnesota and the subsequent nationwide protests, the restaurant announced that it would change the name from Sambo's due to community demands and an online petition signed by more than four thousand people. The petition was created by Santa Barbara resident Rashelle Monet. The owner, Chad Stevens, explained to the community why Monet created the petition: "These are challenging times, so we had to step up to the plate. We have had this brand for sixty-five years. I'm covering up as much of it as I can to show respect for Black Lives Matter and the challenges of the African American community."

Later in 2020, Chad Stevens announced to the community and media that the name had been changed from Sambo's to Chad's. He met with Rashelle Monet and discussed the name change, with Monet saying, "It shows we can work together to induce positive change and despite your different backgrounds and different cultures that we can all come together and live together harmoniously."

Street view of the Sambo's on Twenty-Third and Burnside Streets. *Courtesy of photographer Scott Allen Tice.*

The typical colorful interior of a Sambo's restaurant. *Courtesy of photographer Scott Allen Tice.*

There is another restaurant, also called Sambo's, that has existed for more than fifty years but is not affiliated with the large Sambo's chain. This restaurant was originally called Lil' Sambo's and is located in Lincoln City, Oregon. In early July 2020, it was also asked to change the name of its restaurant due to its racial insensitivity. On its website, it issued this statement: "Lil' Sambo's Restaurant has been a coastal landmark for over fifty years. One question we are often asked is whether or not we were ever a part of the Sambo's national chain. The answer is no. Our name is borrowed from the hero of a fictional story about an Indian boy, tigers, and pancakes written by Helen Bannerman in 1899."

One of the most popular Sambo's locations in Portland was on the corner of Twenty-Third and Burnside Street. This location was not the only Sambo's in Portland, as there were several others, including a Sambo's on Eighty-Second Avenue. Along with being open twenty-four hours a day, the Twenty-Third Avenue location served a variety of breakfast and lunch combos with a busy to-go service. Sambo's restaurants sold a large coffee mug that customers could bring with them every day. With the mug, they could get an "endless cup of coffee" for a dime and then later for a quarter. This environmentally conscious idea was a restaurant ploy during the '60s and '70s to lure in customers, and it worked. With the refillable mug of coffee, customers could sit in a booth all day if they wanted. There, they could look out the windows, where the divide between the natural world outside and the orderly interior space within was seemingly bridged.

The color of Sambo's interior décor was generally bright orange but could also be yellow, green and even red in some locations. The Burnside Sambo's had a long section of booths upholstered in springy vinyl situated to the south of the main eating area. The booths overlooked Burnside Street and were roomy and comfortable, with expansive views of fashionable Vista Avenue. To the left of the booths on the other side of the restaurant was the counter, with numerous stools and the warm kitchen directly behind it.

Sitting in a window booth gave customers a feeling of looking out yet being a part of a living stage in motion. Inside the restaurant, customers could watch as people walked down the street, crossed Burnside at the stoplight heading off to work, took their children to school or shopped. Safely ensconced within spacious restaurant booths, customers read for pleasure, studied if they were students or just gazed out the windows and relaxed watching the world go by. The dime cup of coffee kept customers in the restaurant, where inevitably they would open their wallets and buy something else—perhaps pie, ice cream or a lunch or dinner entrée.

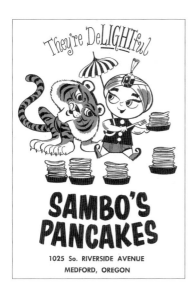

They're DeLIGHTful

SAMBO'S
PANCAKES

1025 So. RIVERSIDE AVENUE
MEDFORD, OREGON

A paper Sambo's menu. *Courtesy of photographer Scott Allen Tice.*

The atmosphere at Sambo's was family friendly and bustling with customers. The smell of good comfort food lingered in the air: the aroma of fresh coffee, vegetable soup, burgers and French fries being the pervasive top notes. The restaurant sold stuffed orange tigers near the cash register, and there were children's coloring books they gave away for free. The tigers were strategically located as people paid their tab and headed out the door, with their children invariably begging parents for their own tiger.

Another appealing visual aspect of the Sambo's chain was the Googie architecture that made the buildings attractive, unique and modern looking. The style became popular in the post–World War II era of the prosperous 1950s and 1960s and used unusual forms and shapes, eye-catching signage, bright colors and a plethora of interesting materials. Googie architecture, as exemplified by the Sambo's restaurants, involved more than just promoting a futuristic look, something similar to *The Jetsons* cartoon show with their images of the atomic age and sleek rocket ships.

The Sambo's structures had specific goals in mind. The buildings used aspects of the architecture of roadside coffee shops, which has also been called Coffee House Modern, Jet Age, Chinese Modern, Doo-Wop, Space Age and Populuxe. Googie architecture as applied to restaurants like Sambo's was strategic and designed to attract motorists who might stop and patronize roadside businesses, such as motels, diners and gas stations: "This new trend required owners and architects to develop a visual imagery so customers would recognize it from the road. This modern consumer architecture was based on communication. This was achieved by using bold style choices, including large pylons with elevated signs, bold neon letters and circular pavilions. Streamline Moderne, much like Googie, was styled to look futuristic to signal the beginning of a new era—that of the automobile and other technologies."

The style got its name, as the story goes, from architecture critic Douglas Haskell, who was a writer for *House and Home Magazine*. The name was originally coined by an American architect named John Edward Lautner

A typical Googie architecture style at Sambo's. *Courtesy of photographer Scott Allen Tice.*

in 1949, when he designed an eye-catching coffee shop. Googie's in Los Angeles was directly adjacent to the famous Schwab's Drugstore, where Hollywood actress Lana Turner was rumored to have been discovered. The name "Googie" had been a family nickname for Lillian K. Burton, the wife of the original owner, Mortimer C. Burton.

When Haskell discovered Googie's, he was driving around Hollywood with photographer Julius Shulman, his friend. Haskell was doing research on a story about colorful coffee shops popping up in the area. Haskell drove by a particular coffee shop at the corner of Sunset Boulevard and Crescent Heights and was immediately impressed with its unique and elegant architecture. It had a bold red roof, linear angles and unexpected curves. Haskell saw that this style of architecture used zigzag roof lines, geometric shapes, upward-sloping roofs, flying saucer and boomerang shapes, sharp angles and exaggerated details. He decided to name the style of architecture after the coffee shop, and with the publication of the *House and Home* article he wrote in 1952, Haskell coined the term "Googie architecture," and it stuck.

Workers in the area of Twenty-Third and Burnside often wanted a quick breakfast and regularly sat at the Sambo's counter, which was closer to the coffee pot and waitresses. In the wide area between the booths and the counter, children would sometimes happily run back and forth after preparing to leave.

The food at this Sambo's was similar to Denny's or an IHOP restaurant, with pancakes, omelets, hash browns, bacon and any number of sandwiches, milkshakes and burger options. People enjoyed the breakfast served all day and being open twenty-four hours made it even more convenient for those working at Good Samaritan Hospital or the Montgomery Ward store or even those working the graveyard or swing shifts at the nearby Esco Steel company farther down on Northwest Vaughn Street.

The national chain was owned by Sam Battistone and Newel Bohnett. Although the name was allegedly created by combining portions of both the owners' first and last names, the chain became associated with *The Story of Little Black Sambo* as a marketing tool and consequently began to suffer because of that often misunderstood connection.

The children's story was originally published in 1899 by Scottish writer Helen Bannerman. *The Story of Little Black Sambo* centers on a resourceful and adventurous young boy from the south of India who outwits a group of hungry tigers. The story was meant to be a positive tale about how children, including children of color, could learn to survive in dangerous circumstances using their intelligence and wits. Bannerman had lived for more than thirty years in India and grew to love the culture and the people. She felt that writing the story could inspire children of all races to become self-sufficient. Bannerman further felt that the stories were meaningful enough to read to her own children:

> *Helen Bannerman (1862–1946) wrote this story during a long railway journey in India, and sent it to her two small daughters whom she had just left to be educated in her native Scotland. It was eventually published as the fourth title in the "Dumpy Books" series, and its success apparently inspired the format of Beatrix Potter's "Peter Rabbit" books. The original publication has gone through countless printings and translations as well as sequels, imitations, and parodies.*

Bannerman also wrote *Little Black Quasha*, *Little Black Mingo* and *Little White Squibba*. Bannerman's stories were not meant to offend any ethnic group, least of all her East Indian friends and neighbors. The illustrations depicting the characters were not considered offensive and were created by Bannerman herself, although it should be noted that Bannerman was *not* a professional artist and could only be described as an amateur illustrator.

The Story of Little Black Sambo was popular with children when it was published in 1899 and even after several pirated editions were illegally published in

Left: The first original drawing of the Sambo's character by Helen Bannerman. *Courtesy of photographer Scott Allen Tice.*

Above: A Sambo's advertisement. *Courtesy of photographer Scott Allen Tice.*

America over the intervening decades. The problems for Sambo's restaurant arose when the pirated editions of the classic story book deviated from the original artwork, which was not offensive. The pirated editions began almost immediately upon the 1899 publication of the book in the UK and spanned more than fifty years of illegal book pirating. This likely occurred because the author was a woman and lived outside the United States.

As the American publishing industry was entirely male dominated at that point, many publishing companies probably presumed that Helen Bannerman and her hugely popular book were fair game, making the pirating of the book simple and lucrative. One such company was the Reilly & Lee Company of Chicago, also known as the Reilly & Britton Company. In its 1908 pirated edition of *Sambo*, the artist was a man named John R. Neil (1877–1943). Neil was a skilled illustrator who was most famous for illustrating thirteen *Wizard of Oz* books written by L. Frank Baum and later nineteen more *Wizard of Oz* books written by Ruth Plumly Thompson. Neil also illustrated a pirated version of *The Story of Little Black Sambo*, and it was his exaggerated and offensive illustrations that were typical of many such images of the Sambo's story that became objectionable to African Americans and white Americans as well.

The new illustrations of the pirated books depicted grotesque and exaggerated illustrations of the character Sambo as an African American child instead of a child from South India. Many Americans rightly considered the illustrations insulting and denigrating to people of color. The pirated editions were used without the legal permission of the original publisher, Grant Richards of London, England, or of any surviving family of Helen Bannerman.

Part of the offensive nature of the name Sambo is also because the word is an old and derogatory term for a person of color or a person of mixed heritage. Examples of the term being used as a derogatory name can be found going back to the nineteenth century. In the 1847 novel *Vanity Fair* by William Makepeace Thackeray, one of the characters is a dark-skinned Indian servant of the Sedley family and is called Sambo. Furthermore, in the novel *Uncle Tom's Cabin* by Harriet Beecher Stowe, an overseer is also called Sambo. And there have been numerous documented occasions when the term was used as a stereotypical name for African Americans going back to the time of the Civil War. As a result, the term "Sambo" is considered a racially insensitive and offensive slur.

By the early 1960s, both Black and white Americans were offended by the name of the Sambo's restaurant chain and began to protest with letters and telephone calls. The restaurant responded by changing the skin color of the illustrations of the boy character to that of a lighter-skinned boy wearing a jewel-laden turban instead of a darker-skinned boy.

By 1979, there were a total of 1,117 Sambo's restaurants in forty-seven American states. Controversy over the chain's name drew even more volatile protests, including lawsuits from individuals and community groups. Several new Sambo's restaurants set to open were quickly renamed the Jolly Tiger. This happened in cities where community organizations forbade the use of the original name or refused to grant the chain permits to operate if they attempted to use the name Sambo's.

The once popular Sambo's restaurant chain had used the 1899 Helen Bannerman story and modified images of the original illustrations to promote and decorate its restaurants, fostering the idea that children could be resourceful, including children of color. But the name "Sambo" was simply too loaded a term. The negative connection to the term was the reason the restaurant chain began shuttering one location after another beginning in the early 1980s.

One common thread in online social media discussions regarding the Sambo's restaurant chain is that some white persons often do not understand the reasoning behind why the term is offensive, or of its history or derogatory usage in literature and during the Civil War. They generally believe that the combining of the two original owners' names to create the restaurant name, or the connection to the children's book with the Indian character, is proof that the name Sambo's is not an offensive racial slur.

On the other hand, most African Americans and other enlightened Americans have a better understanding of the history of the term. They understand how it was used derogatorily in literature and during the Civil War as a racial slur directed at Black soldiers and why it is an unsuitable name for a modern restaurant. Bridging this gap in perceptions should be a goal toward gaining a better understanding why the term *is* and *was* an unacceptable racial slur.

Despite the chain's many problems with the name and public outcry, Sambo's was plagued with other problems as well, which ended up impacting the chain financially. This included how corporate-level management did business. Employees of Sambo's wanted to be treated more equitably and paid better. Managers wanted better compensation packages and struggled for years to achieve that with little success.

The company had a promotion that began in the mid-1970s called "fraction of the action." This was a manager-partnership program acting as an incentive and "capital generating idea largely responsible for Sambo's early success." Managers were entitled to 20 percent of all profits. They could purchase up to an additional 30 percent interest in 5 percent increments. Employees were allowed to bid for a percentage of the remaining profits as well. It was an early company expansion plan, and the growth of the company quickly outpaced its control. Proceeds from the "action units" were included in the income statement of managers and other employees, and this became important for Sambo's bottom line.

The chains were expanding rapidly, and it became difficult to add stores at a quicker rate so that earnings from these programs could continue to rise. The incentives sounded incredibly appealing to all the employees, with everyone having a stake in the final outcome, but some of the managers could take no time off and were working seven days a week. Then, in the fall of 1977, the Securities and Exchange Commission had some unwelcome news for management, telling them that they "could not record 'fraction-of-the action' receipts as sales since Sambo's retained the right to buy back participations when managers left the company. Thereafter, Sambo's eliminated the program and profits were severely affected as disgruntled managers left the company in large numbers."

In a desperate attempt to save the chain and create a new image, the corporate powers in March 1981 changed the names of some of the locations to No Place Like Sam's, but the name change just didn't work. The stain of the racial slur connected to the name Sambo's could not be forgotten. By November 1981, the company had filed for bankruptcy. The name change and the bankruptcy could not reverse the downward spiral, and by 1982, all Sambo's restaurants other than the original location had closed. By February 1983, 618 of the locations had been renamed Season's Friendly Eating, and several others had been sold to the Denny's chain.

The West Burnside Sambo's had a long and interesting run. Many Portlanders remember their family outings, as well as other more interesting and sometimes comical incidents. Sandy Moose, longtime wife of the late PPB police chief Charles Moose, remembered when she worked there. While Sandy attended the Power's Modeling School at nights, she worked at Sambo's and remembered that sometimes food safety was not always a high priority, with unsafe food handling practices at times regularly overlooked: "I worked at Sambo's in 1971 and 1972. The restaurant had a big vat of mixed pancake batter just behind the swinging doors out of public view back in the kitchen. It didn't have a lid on it, and on more than one occasion the dishwasher spit in the vat. It was gross. I quit before I got fired."

Kane Hannam, a longtime Portlander, remembered going to the Burnside Sambo's with his mother when he was ten years old for lunch one afternoon. His mother remarked to him that the cook was not wearing a hairnet, and she sure hoped she didn't find a hair in her food—"That would be it!" his mother said. Sadly, as she ate her lunch she stopped suddenly, and Kane remembered thinking, "Oh boy!" knowing that it would not be good. "Sure enough, about halfway through her sandwich her face became this gray paralyzed façade. She flips open her sandwich to inspect the components and loudly starts retching. And by loud I mean my mom could have put the wolves on Mount Hood off their food. She goes running to the restroom, retching the entire way. I was left in the booth, mortified and trying my best to blend in with what I remember was an awful greenish Naugahyde."

Many other Portlanders remember happy times at Sambo's. Greg Meier recalled how much he enjoyed the Burnside Sambo's location when he went there with his family for breakfast and lunch as a child: "I loved that place! They had a coloring book and crayons that they gave to kids. It told the story of the little boy Sambo in India and a tiger. It was kind of like the *Jungle Book*. You got to color in the book and take it home."

Longtime Portlander Robin Crandall recalled an amusing, stereotypically '70s incident that occurred as she and her family were headed to the Oregon coast and stopped off at Sambo's first:

It was the early 1970s, and we were on our way to our beach house late one night. My Dad stopped to get coffee to go for the long trip. We pulled into the Sambo's parking lot to the right that went around the back. At about the same time, a van pulled up next to us, and four young men jumped out, sans any clothes but shoes. They sprinted around the entire perimeter of the restaurant, jumped back in the idling van and took off. That was my first experience ever seeing streakers. I can only imagine what the restaurant patrons did when this occurred, with those big plate glass windows looking out onto Burnside Street.

Several companies and restaurants have now joined Sambo's as examples of brand name death because of the derogatory nature of their depictions of race in America and the hurtful impact it has on people of color. Although the original owners of Sambo's opened their restaurant with good intentions, the offensive name led to the chain's demise, and it became a lesson to all, including those working in the advertising industry, that the power of language and illustration is immense and can either make or break a business.

CLUB 21, 1958–2017

The cozy building formerly located at 2035 Northeast Glisan Street, off Sandy—the building that became Club 21—was not always a restaurant. Located in the Kerns neighborhood, the building was originally believed to be a Russian Orthodox church. With its quaint castle-like façade, red chateau-esque roof and bright whitewashed exterior, the rumor was an often-repeated misinterpretation of the building's original history. Who started the rumor is unknown, but the belief that the building began as a church has proven to be false.

According to Deacon David Cole of the Holy Trinity Greek Orthodox Cathedral in Portland, the building "never, ever was a church." Cole is an expert on the history of Russian churches and their funding and construction, going back some one hundred years. He has stated unequivocally that the structure was not a Russian church. The history of the old building is a bit more mundane.

What is certain regarding the structure that became Club 21 is that in 1926, Century Investment Company acquired a ninety-nine-year lease for the full block bounded by Northeast Twentieth and Twenty-First and Glisan and Hoyt Streets. In 1929, construction began on a new "tea room" for the

Exterior image of the Club 21. © *Thomas Robinson.*

Jack and Jill All Pure Ice Cream Company. The location of the structure was on the corner of East Twenty-First and Glisan and was described as being a "Mission style with a shake exterior." The company that built the structure was Reimers & Jolivette. Established in 1922, it is known for its "craftsmanship" and excellent work restoring old houses and buildings to their original glory. Reimers & Jolivette remains in operation to this day.

An *Oregonian* article from March 1929 reported that Jack and Jill Ice Cream was set to open and would be doing business in a newly constructed "English type cottage." An *Oregon Journal* article from the following month reported that the ice cream shop had opened at Twenty-First and Glisan Streets and that the manager was a man named J.E. Hawkins, who also managed the Jack and Jill Ice Cream shop located in downtown Portland. Mysteriously, the new ice cream shop didn't do well and closed after eight weeks. In another *Oregon Journal* article dated June 18, 1929, workers are mentioned as "remodeling the new building" for a restaurant, which meant including several thousand dollars' worth of new restaurant equipment. In yet another *Oregonian* article from June 23, 1929, it is revealed that Jake's Famous Crawfish would be taking over the new lease from the Century Investment Company and that the building was indeed originally "erected for a restaurant."

The original myth that the building was a church may be the result of simple rumor and word of mouth relating to the appearance of the structure. It is plausible the rumor began because the building operated as a Russian café called the Samovar Café during the 1930s. Portlanders may have been confused by the appearance of the building and the Russians who frequented the café with religious people—Russians at that time in Portland often dressed in traditional Russian garb for holidays and weddings. The assumption that the building had been a church has persisted for decades, and several Portland newspapers, even as recently as 2017, have repeated the error even after Club 21 was shuttered.

The church rumor may be connected to documents from the Portland Archives and Records Center, which indicate that the building was used from 1943 to 1944 during World War II for what was simply called the "St. Apostolic Church." If the building was not used as a place of worship, due to the obvious small size of the structure, it could have acted as a temporary rectory or in another supporting role, perhaps as a service center or food charity. Unfortunately, there are no other corroborating records or documentation that shed additional light on the one year that the building was used in connection to what was simply called the St. Apostolic Church.

Before it became Club 21, it was the Samovar Café. *Courtesy of photographer Scott Allen Tice.*

OPENING TODAY

Now an

EAST SIDE BRANCH
E. 21st St. and Glisan at Sandy

For 13 years Jake has been serving those famous crawfish of his, known all over the world, to thousands at the cafe on 12th and Stark. Jake's has become a landmark in Portland . . . the bright spot for after-theater parties.

The new branch will be a most welcome addition to scores of Portlanders and their friends. It is modern, handsomely appointed and a pleasant place to adjourn to when your parties break up.

Remember the New Jake's Place

East 21st and Glisan
AT SANDY

The short-lived East Side Branch by Jake's Famous Crawfish. *Courtesy of photographer Scott Allen Tice.*

Restaurateur Jacob Lewis Freiman was born in Portland in 1865 and spent his youth growing up in The Dalles, Oregon. He returned to Portland at the age of twenty-seven to open up Jake's Famous Crawfish in 1892 at its flagship location, where it remains open today on Southwest Stark Street in downtown Portland. Years later, Freiman, along with his partner, Clem F. Hackman, opened up a second location at 2035 Northeast Glisan, in the same building that would become Club 21. The grand opening of what they called Jake's Eastside Bungalow occurred on June 2, 1929. This second Jake's location, much like the ice cream parlor venture, didn't take off. This could have been because the east side location may not have been a wise choice due to the populations of lower-income Portlanders living there.

Another newspaper article explained, "During the Great Depression of the 1930s, Jake's had to close this east side location in order to remain solvent." The poor location led to a financial loss, and Freiman and Hackman were forced to close their new restaurant sometime in the early 1930s. Strangely, the same archived records that indicated the building was used by a church from 1943 to 1944 also claim that the building was used by the owner of Jake's Famous Crawfish for yet another go at a restaurant in 1932. This time, the restaurant was called Jake's Shellfish, but again, this restaurant did not take off and was closed down; the building remained unused and vacant all during 1933.

Later, in 1934, the building became the Samovar Café. It was operated by Paul George Bulkin (1894–1971), a native of Moscow. The Samovar "introduced Russian cuisine and Russian entertainment to a receptive Portland clientele." Bulkin and his bride, Frances Elizabeth Hulshizer, had their wedding ceremony and reception at the Samovar Café on June 16, 1934. The Samovar operated for a bit over seven years before closing in 1941. It catered to a mostly Russian American customer base. With the Jantzen factory nearby (formerly called the Portland Knitting Company) and the large population of Russian immigrant employees working there, the Samovar Café is said to have been quite popular. The Russian Jantzen employees must have been happy to have a slice of the homeland nearby where they could enjoy their native cuisine and mix with family and friends.

After the Samovar Café closed in 1941 and the building was used from 1943 to 1944 by the St. Apostolic Church, there are long stretches where there are no known records on what businesses may have occupied the building. However, a restaurant called Wieser's Restaurant is also documented to have occupied the space at some point. Eventually, the building became known as the Shadows Night Club in 1950. It was then renamed the New Shadows Night Club in 1955, and from 1959 to 1960, it was called the Shadows Restaurant. The name was probably a reference to the dim interior of the building. After the restaurant was shuttered, the building would finally bear the name Club 21.

The original owners of Club 21, Sam A. Nicoletti and Dave Nudo, did business for thirty years before Club 21 was taken over by new owners in the early 1990s. Prior to 1961, Nicoletti had begun working in the restaurant business with one of his cousins, opening up Nick's Coney Island on Southeast Hawthorne Street. Soon after that, Nicoletti decided to partner with Nudo and open Club 21.

Although it changed hands several times, the name of the restaurant remained Club 21 for fifty-nine years. The restaurant went through numerous management changes and was mostly known during the 1960s and 1970s as an old man's bar. Having developed the reputation as a place where elderly sailors and other retired military men tended to gather to drink and enjoy the steaks for which Club 21 was once known, it slowly morphed into a place popular with young people and metal bands during the 1990s and into the 2000s.

Still intact on the west side of the roof, erected when it was the Shadows Nightclub or perhaps Wieser's Restaurant, one could see the prominent signage with the words "Steaks for Your Enjoyment," and this became the

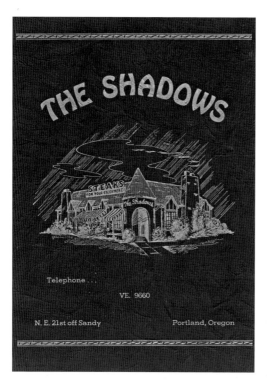

Left: A menu from when the business was called The Shadows. *Courtesy of photographer Scott Allen Tice.*

Below: A typical sandwich, tots and coffee from Club 21. *Courtesy of photographer Scott Allen Tice.*

catchphrase for newspaper and radio advertisements, promoting Club 21 as a place known for high-quality steaks. Food was simple at Club 21, but its steaks remained notable during its early days, until it stopped serving them sometime in the 2000s.

In the '90s, Club 21 offered brunch seven days a week and happy hour specials from 3:00 p.m. to 7:00 p.m., along with hearty breakfast, lunch and dinner menus. After the once sedate Club 21 became a hipster hangout, it eventually earned the reputation as a local dive bar, known for having good chili and great burgers and sandwiches.

Over the years, the décor changed from understated '60s elegance to random garage sale chaos. When customers walked beneath the arch and through the front door, there were tables and booths, along with seats at the bar. The interior looked something like a lodge of sorts, with mounted deer heads, wood-paneled walls, velvet paintings of busty half-naked women and dozens of vintage beer signs. There were Demolition Man and Judge Dredd pinball machines, stuffed animals, strangely crafted dioramas, eerie antique dolls, a creepy snakeskin nailed to the wall, two flat-screen televisions to watch the latest sports game and a digital jukebox with music as varied as the Violent Femmes and Johnny Cash. The interior sported all manner of other amusing bric-a-brac, which decorated every inch of the kitschy interior, including a large gas log fireplace with a gas log that was able to heat the interior on cold days.

Despite Club 21 having developed a shabby appearance, it was still beloved by the locals in the Kerns neighborhood. Outside in the back, there was a good-sized patio behind a privacy wall with umbrellas where folks could assemble, eat, drink and people watch. The patio was known to be dog friendly, with bowls of fresh water set out during the warm months. In winter, the patio had several heat lamps to keep customers cozy, with smoking allowed. The tables were mismatched and of varying sizes, so a couple could have a table in relative privacy or a large group could be seated together. The beer selection at Club 21 was always good and affordable but not extensive, and of course, there was a full bar at all times, including a ten-dollar "bottomless Mimosa" that was popular.

One aspect of the menu during its last few years in operation was the build-a-burger concept. With a plastic laminated menu and an erasable pen, you could create your own burger. In about fifteen to twenty minutes, your unique burger would appear before you. The build-a-burger menu contained a total of fifty-three ingredients. This included meatless burger options, gluten-free buns, sharp white cheddar cheese and crisp bacon. It also offered fresh tomatoes, raw chopped onions, smoked gouda, sautéed caramelized whiskey onions, grilled pineapple, fried egg, roasted red peppers and maple ham, along with its popular Club 21 Special Sauce.

The meat was Painted Hills ground chuck, known as "grass fed" beef. Sides were plentiful and included French fries, onion rings and its popular deep-fried pickles. It had the Smoky Pepper Barbecue Chicken Burger, the Pineapple Teriyaki Jalapeño Veggie Burger and the Tomato Bacon-Jam Burger. The signature Club 21 Burger was made with bacon, one crisp onion ring, lettuce, tomato-bacon jam and an impressive slab of smoked gouda cheese.

Anna Mehrer recalled the vast scope of those who visited Club 21 and how far-reaching that could be: "I went to high school in Germany from 1987 to 1990 and would babysit from time to time, so, fast-forward to 2015. I'm sitting on the patio at Club 21 one night. A couple of people ask if they could share the table. I say sure, and a couple of beats later, I ask the man, 'Are you Andrew?' He replies, 'Yeah!' to which I say, 'I used to babysit you in Bonn. Last time I saw you, you were in diapers!' It was such a Portland moment, but it happened at Club 21!"

Dennis Vigna worked at Club 21 for five years and remembered the good times: "Dave Nudo, my cousin, was part owner of Club 21. Dave was the epitome of a great bartender. He had everyone's attention when he worked the bar. He drew in all walks of life to Club 21, from CEOs, politicians, famous sport athletes to everyday people. He treated everyone the same. He attracted bar owners from all over Portland back in the day. The five years I worked there contain priceless memories for me."

Club 21 was particularly loved by the many people who lived within walking distance, as well as the KATU employees, who often came by for lunch, dinner and drinks after they got off their shifts and needed a place to relax and unwind. Corky Miller, retired cameraman with KATU, remembered Club 21 as the place to go after a hard day or night at work: "It was the principal debriefing spot for Channel 2 News. I can't remember in my thirteen years as a cameraman all of the stories and newscasts we would come down from while at Club 21. Mount St. Helens, Tonya Harding, the '96 floods, Diane Downs, elections nights! I even had a few drink sessions with Bill O'Reilly there when he was an anchor at KATU."

Club 21 was known for having what some people described as "the strongest drinks in town." Courtney Sherwood remembered how potent those drinks could be: "They used to pour the stiffest drinks in town. Once, my ex-husband ordered a double whiskey, and they filled a twelve-ounce cup to the top with no ice. We lived down the street, so we sneaked out with the unfinished drink and he eventually got through it over several days."

Yelp and other online review sites often included amusing entries. Kimberly V. of Portland wrote in 2008 on Yelp, "Proud sign on the roof says 'Steaks for your enjoyment.' It doesn't mention the lung cancer. Club 21 gives you both, plus booze."

In 2008, Jenny H. of Portland wrote, "Please don't change, Club 21. You're there when we need you, like when it gets too rowdy at the Slut [The Sandy Hut] or I get a mean hankering for tots after midnight. Your lumpy booths are charming, and I can't get over the wee flat-screen TVs now installed at each booth! Also I like that you sound vaguely strip-clubby and look like an enchanted castle in the middle of a parking lot."

There were a lot of diehard Club 21 fans, including Jess P. of Washington, D.C., who wrote on Yelp, "This place is seedy. I like it! Poorly lit, a plethora of pinball machines, half-cleared tables. Of course, true to Portland, this bar proves that bar food can be something close to spectacular. The menu hosts your staples—wings, burgers, and greasy fried things. But it gets creative. There's fun sauces, there's a build your own burger, there's rainier-battered onion rings. Vegheads—the veggie burger is outstanding. Anaheim peppers, chipotle mayo, pepper-jack cheese—wow. For the meat eaters—even more choices, I'm sure you'll walk away quite pleased."

But nothing lasts forever. In a short online article from January 9, 2017, Mattie John Bamman wrote, "Portland Dive Bar that Looks like Snow White's House Officially Doomed. Bye-Bye Beloved Club 21." Sharing the sad news that Club 21 would soon be demolished, the article continued: "One of Portland's most historic and iconic dive bars—if you're driving on Northeast Sandy it's pretty near impossible to miss—Club 21 has been on the chopping block for years, and now *The Mercury* reports the end is officially here. Co-owner Warren Boothby says moving the venue isn't feasible (the one-of-a-kind structure wouldn't survive the trip), and Club 21 will close for good on January 15. It's the latest Portland institution to be demolished in the wake of the city's real estate boom."

The last owners, Marcus Archambeault and Boothby, tried valiantly to keep Club 21 open, but it was not to be. They had wanted to move the "distinctive witch house" building to a vacant lot. Archambeault was saddened and said, "We gave it a really good try. If I owned the land I would keep the club there forever."

The property was purchased several times by developers who knew that the structure was in poor condition and pushed for its demolition because

Left: Club 21 after it had closed and been vandalized. *Courtesy of photographer Scott Allen Tice.*

Right: The old Club 21 sign ("Steaks for your enjoyment") being taken to The Vern, where it is now hangs on a wall inside. *Courtesy of photographer Scott Allen Tice.*

they wanted to develop the lot. They became more and more aggressive and continued to raise the monthly rent. Although the owners tried hard to keep Club 21 open, they were not successful, and it was shuttered after fifty-nine long and eventful years. There was an immediate outpouring of rebuke and unhappiness among longtime Portlanders that yet another restaurant would come under the wrecking ball. People began pouring in shortly before Club 21 shuttered to party, take photographs and get a last glimpse and a last drink at their beloved Club 21.

The land was purchased by Los Angeles cable tycoon and real estate billionaire Marc Nathanson and was turned into a 212-unit mixed-use apartment complex called the Jantzen Apartments. Although Club 21 was demolished and is gone forever, the memory of the funny little "Snow White's House" on the corner of Glisan and Sandy, with its unique and varied history and quaint castle-like appearance, will continue to live on in stories of the fabled dives that once helped define Portland's weirdness. After the old building was dismantled, the steak sign, famous for decades as it rested on the roof of Club 21, was taken down and shipped over to The Vern to be displayed inside its establishment for all to see as a final nod to Portland's beloved Club 21.

THE BURGER BARN, 1959–1994

The building that eventually became the Burger Barn restaurant was formerly located at 3962 Northeast Martin Luther King Boulevard. The now demolished building has a fascinating and historically significant connection to Portland history that is worth recording. Not only is the history important to recall for the sake of Portland's posterity, but also for the thousands of Portland citizens and out-of-state visitors who have fond memories of eating and socializing at the Burger Barn.

The original address, before the streets were renumbered (addresses all through Portland were altered during the early 1930s), was 840 Union Avenue North. The structure was a humble wood-frame building built in 1900 and created as a workspace for trade businesses. As such, it was one of the oldest buildings in the area. On the north side of the building was a small addition that likely incorporated a modest living area in the east corner, located to the rear of the building. The west corner of that addition had a large window that was used for displays and to advertise the occupying business and attract customers. At some point over the years, that small addition was removed for unknown reasons, and the building became a simple boxlike structure still perfectly suited for tradesmen to work in, or even as a home for a small family.

The Burger Barn was originally a merchant building. © *Thomas Robinson.*

The backstory of the Burger Barn's building deserves some recognition, particularly in that it was the home to the notable Portland Black suffrage pioneer Katherine Gray, who arrived in Portland with her husband, Harry M. Gray, and their four children in 1900. Gray's husband is listed on census records as working as a gold miner, among other occupations, during his relatively short life. The family moved into the building that would later become the Burger Barn in 1906 and lived and worked there until either 1911 or possibly as late as 1917. Gray founded the Harriet Tubman Club and acted as one of the founders of the Zion African Methodist Episcopal (AME) Church in Portland, located on North Vancouver.

Gray volunteered as an active member of the Colored Women's Equal Suffrage Club, working alongside Harriet "Hattie" Redmond, who was the most recognized and influential of all the Black suffrage leaders in early Portland. Hattie Redmond's father was the beloved Reuben Crawford, who worked as a skilled ship caulker and endeared himself to many in Portland with his excellent craftsmanship and warm personality. Crawford was an emancipated slave, as was his wife, Redmond's mother, Lavinia. Reuben Crawford was active in the Republican Lincoln Club and with the Portland Colored Immigration Society and encouraged all of his eight children to excel and achieve.

Gray and Redmond were also involved with the Colored Women's Council of Portland, with Gray becoming vice-president in 1914, while her daughter Edith acted as secretary. The Colored Women's Council helped alleviate poverty and hardship among Black Portland residents who struggled. Specifically, it was known for helping "poor and unfortunate women" with food, clothing and other necessities. It did this to help make the lives of struggling Black women more manageable and hopeful at a time when the power structure in Portland demonstrated callous indifference and frightening racism to people of color. Katherine Gray and Hattie Redmond raised money for scholarships, read together, promoted education in the Black community and even created book clubs where they could get together and discuss literature and politics. Gray was one of the most important Black activists in Portland's early history. She helped shape the history of the city in a powerful way due to her admirable efforts to create positive social change and advocate for Black families and Black women specifically.

The building was later used by several tradesmen during the 1930s. The first on record was a man named George Thaut, a Russian immigrant born in 1877 who worked as a shoemaker. Later, there was a jeweler named Edgar McCreary, a tailor named Alec Weitzel and another tailor named John Hunt.

The Burger Barn, circa 1980s. © *Thomas Robinson.*

Hunt worked in the building all during the 1930s before finally moving across the street, where he continued his tailoring business until 1963.

During the 1950s, the building became the site of several cafés. The first on record was the Cat N' Fiddle Café, followed by Dean's Café and then, around 1959, the Burger Barn. This final establishment was owned and operated by George Washington Powe and his wife, Geraldine Raiford Powe, along with various family members who often helped out.

During the years the Burger Barn was in operation, it became a place where Black Americans in the Portland community could meet and spend time together, eat good food and share the news of the day. The food served at the Burger Barn was considered good soul food and was popular with residents of every race. George Powe, originally from Memphis, Tennessee, and his wife, Geraldine, were known for their excellent barbecue pork ribs (which sometimes took a full hour to prepare), along with their delicious oxtail stew, collard greens, black-eyed peas, candied yams and full roast beef dinners.

The success of the Burger Barn was directly linked to Geraldine Powe, a strikingly attractive woman of Creole descent. Mrs. Powe's "Mississippi roots" and expert understanding of food preparation, fresh produce, seafood and baking made her a legend in the North End for creating bona fide "soul food" that everyone in Portland could enjoy. She maintained a garden; she also bred chickens, made wine and made each dish or dessert for the Burger Barn strictly from scratch, including their famous barbecue and hot sauce, which was never store bought.

The Burger Barn menu had the popular chicken basket and the wing basket along with cheeseburgers. It also had a fish basket and a shrimp basket, as well as the ever-present pot of good strong coffee that went well with its desserts of homemade banana pudding, served with wafers and whipped cream, and its freshly baked sweet potato pies.

One longtime customer, AJ Calhoun, remembered the barbecue pork ribs and its special sauce: "I went there several times for lunch. It took an hour to prepare the pork ribs. The sauce was complex and wonderful. One of the best I ever tasted. I romanticize it as a sauce that was both spicy and sweet. I'm sure there was vinegar and red pepper and tomato, but also sugar and garlic. It wasn't the usual thick brown barbecue sauce. With all the different cuisine we have today, it was somewhere between Thai and Caribbean. It was a long time ago, but I've never tasted anything quite like it again. I remember their barbecue chicken, and it was great too. When Red's BBQ came to town, it was all the rage, but their sauce was nothing close to the Burger Barn sauce!"

Another fan of the Burger Barn remembered the days he spent recovering from a night out drinking: "They had the best fried chicken in the city! It was damn good food cooked with a ton of love. Mrs. Geraldine Powe was the mother a lot of customers never had."

As the restaurant was open all night, Portland police officers often stopped by for coffee and cheeseburgers if they were working the graveyard shift. The Burger Barn was one of the only places open twenty-four hours a day, and Don DuPay remembered frequenting the restaurant beginning in 1961 as a young police officer. At that time, an officer didn't have to pay for coffee in most restaurants, but DuPay, having grown up in the restaurant business, took offense at that exploitative tradition and chose to pay for his coffee, which confused more than one waitress working at the Burger Barn: "I always paid for my coffee at the Burger Barn and for the food too. The people of Albina at that time were not used to seeing cops pay for their coffee, but I did it because it was the right thing to do. Running a restaurant is a challenge, and I had empathy for them. I remember how hard it was for my parents when they operated DuPay's Drive-In Restaurant over on McLoughlin. I always paid my way. Not all the officers did though, and I knew that, too."

In the 1950s and 1960s, many restaurants considered free coffee a tradeoff they were willing to accept. Police officers came in, got free coffee and sometimes even free burgers, and the restaurant benefited from the presence of law enforcement officers hanging around who could chase away any potential troublemakers. For the most part, this attitude was prevalent at the Burger Barn during the 1960s, but it began to shift in the 1970s and

1980s when racial tensions between the Black community in Portland and the Portland Police Bureau grew.

The Burger Barn did great business for a long time and was not a source of disturbance or controversy during the 1960s, as remembered by DuPay. The citizens and the police officers, according to DuPay, sat across from one another in the small interior space and never intruded on one another. The restaurant provided good hot coffee and quality food, becoming a place to get out of the cold and the various dangers of the Portland night.

As time went on, particularly as the 1980s progressed, the Burger Barn began to experience the changes of a shifting social and political landscape, and occasionally there were disturbances in or around the restaurant, including criminal activity. Fred Stewart, longtime Portland real estate broker, remembered that things could sometimes get dicey:

> *The Burger Barn was one of the places pimps hung out during the winter to keep warm while their girls were freezing and pulling tricks on Union Avenue. There was the Winchell's Donut Shop, which is now Geneva's. You had the Burger Barn and Denny's. The difference between Winchell's and the Burger Barn location is there are more ghosts. Quite a few people got killed in front of the Burger Barn or close to it. These were men who were criminals because those were the best options for a lot of black men of their generation. And at one time in this community, some of what they were doing was useful. As things changed, there were more opportunities for black people in Portland and that included the opportunity to sell their property and move away to where you* wanted *to live.*

Another Portlander, Jim Pilcher, a taxi driver at the time, remembered the Burger Barn and the area near it: "You had to go a long way to find a worse neighborhood back in the '80s. Empty houses, gangs, shootings nightly, all the drugs you could eat. It got better when the *Oregonian* hit the banks for redlining and once people moved back into the empty houses."

Unfortunately, in 1981, the Burger Barn became the scene of an unprovoked attack of racism against the Black owners, George and Geraldine Powe. The attack became symbolic of the police harassment that Black folks living in the North End often experienced at the hands of certain radicalized Portland police officers. The incident became emblematic of what Black Portlanders endured due to racism within the police bureau and sparked a huge response from Portland citizens of all colors.

The Powe family and the entire Black community became outraged when on the night of March 12, 1981, several Portland police officers dumped a number of dead opossums at the front door of the Burger Barn in full view of several witnesses. George Powe was interviewed by KATU News and expressed his concern that the harassment by police would not end but only get worse. The police said that the attack was not based on racism but was just due to police officers blowing off steam from the stressors of the job, but the Black community and many in the white community in Portland did not buy that excuse.

Officers Craig Ward and Jim Gallaway admitted that as they were patrolling North Precinct, they dumped several dead opossums on the sidewalk in front of the Burger Barn. Later, as documented by an arbitrator's report, Ward admitted that he had killed two animals by running them over with his patrol car. Whether this was accidental or intentional was not made public. Then, according to the report, Ward and Gallaway located three more of the unfortunate animals and shockingly clubbed them to death with their batons. No practical reason was ever provided as to why this inhumane and callous act was done to the innocent animals, but after contacting eight to ten other officers, Ward and Gallaway met in an adjacent parking lot near the Burger Barn and were seen dumping the dead opossums while other officers watched.

The Powe family stated that the Portland police had engaged in "a conspiracy to deprive them of their constitutional rights." As a result of the incident and their subsequent reporting of it, the Powe family stated that they had received "threatening phone calls and the police have flashed their patrol lights into their home." The Powe family stated also that they suffered "emotional distress and continued to fear for their own safety and that of their family and friends, and that they will continue to suffer as a consequence of being targeted for racial discrimination."

The Powe family sought $2.8 million in punitive damages, claiming that the acts by police were indeed the result of maliciousness and racist ill will toward them, but in the end they were awarded only $64,000.

The family, as represented by Wilsonville lawyer Michael Kohlhoff, went a step further and sought "an injunction to prohibit the city from continuing to maintain any policy or practice of racial discrimination or harassment." To accomplish that goal, the Powe family requested the courts to order the city to submit a plan, which would be approved by the court and would provide "additional education, training and monitoring of police functions."

George Powe was interviewed on camera with KATU and said that he'd been getting harassing phone calls from people he believed to be police officers, asking such things as, "You got any possum stew?" One of his sons witnessed the original March 12 event and claimed that there were *ten* officers involved in the act and believed that the Portland Police Bureau and city officials did not do enough to investigate the incident fully. If only two were identified as being involved, that left another eight who could freely harass Powe and his family as they tried to operate their small restaurant.

Powe also stated to KATU reporters that the witnesses who saw the incident unfold were never allowed to look at photographs of other officers so that they might be able to identify them. And again Powe claimed that the bureau and city officials were attempting to protect the other officers' identities by essentially sweeping the incident under the rug.

Longtime Portland resident, businessman, community activist and cable access TV talk show host Bruce Broussard was so angered by the incident that he organized a march to city hall. Broussard was accompanied by many Black residents and a large number of white Portlanders as well, angry over the incident and what it conveyed to the Black community. Broussard was in direct communication with the mayor and police chief as he organized the march, to communicate to the Portland Police Bureau that this kind of racism in Portland would no longer be tolerated by the Black community.

Years later, Craig Ward described the incident: "It was the biggest mistake of my life. I put the city through hell and brought discredit to the bureau. But it wasn't done out of meanness or racial motivation. It's my fault, and I try to make amends for it every day." This claim, though conciliatory in tone, is difficult for many Portlanders to accept, even decades later. Many reason that if the incident had not been racially motivated, why did the officers target a Black-owned restaurant, rather than a white-owned restaurant, of which there were far more in Portland at the time?

Sadly, the Burger Barn was shuttered around 1994, with no media comment from any Portland newspapers. Portland lost not only an important restaurant but also a slice of Portland history, one where people of color could gather and enjoy genuine soul food made from scratch, a place people from all over the Portland area had grown to love.

THE BARBARY COAST/HOYT HOTEL, 1962–1972

The Barbary Coast Restaurant and Lounge began operating within the interior of the Hoyt Hotel decades after the hotel was built. The Hoyt Hotel was a 175-room structure built in 1917 and situated on the southwest corner of Northwest Sixth and Broadway, a block south of Union Station. For decades, the Hoyt housed tens of thousands of Portland renters and out-of-state travelers as a simple hotel with moderate to poor accommodations. With its choice location, the Hoyt was popular during the heyday of passenger rail travel and was always bustling with activity. As the trains rumbled into town, the Hoyt Hotel was the first hotel passengers saw after stepping off the train to explore the city.

Portland businessman Harvey Dick (1904–1977) purchased the hotel in 1941 and continued renting rooms, primarily as housing for wartime steel workers. As a descendant from a wealthy banking family, Dick is best remembered for having been part owner of Columbia Steel and for owning and operating the Hoyt Hotel and the Barbary Coast restaurant. Dick arranged the colorful entertainment venues at the Barbary Coast and at Harvey's Comedy Club. The comedy club was originally named Harvey's Bar and was named in honor of Harvey Dick.

After the Hoyt had been in business several decades, it became run-down and was considered a "fleabag hotel," used mainly by common laborers looking for work. Despite being worse for wear, in 1961 Dick decided to invest $2 million toward renovating the old building. When all was said and done, Dick had created the Barbary Coast Restaurant and Lounge and the Roaring 20s Room, which was a nightclub and known for attracting celebrities like Duke Ellington, Johnny Carson and Annie Francis.

The Barbary Coast restaurant became one of Portland's hottest gathering places for well-heeled and regular working-class Portlanders. People went there to be seen and to socialize in the large, sprawling restaurant and lounge, both decorated in creative and quirky historic décor. It's difficult to say what look Dick was looking for, but it ended up being an eclectic mishmash that people seemed to enjoy.

The restaurant even had a glass meat case where customers could look over the various cuts of meat so they could decide which steak they wanted cooked on the grill for their dinner. The radio station KLIQ had its studio in the hotel lobby and was a source of constant activity, entertainment and advertising.

The historic Hoyt Hotel, circa 1970s. © *Thomas Robinson*.

The popularity of the Barbary Coast was due in part to the fact that it was open twenty-four hours a day as well as to the Early American Revival, which occurred in popular culture during the 1960s. Guests were treated to a trip back in time with the nostalgic décor of the "Gay Nineties." Many ornate furnishings came from the Old West era of the 1880s and provided the literal props needed to take that trip down memory lane. The appearance of the interior of the Barbary Coast and Roaring 20s Room created an alluring ambiance of romance and daring adventure—a kind of fantasy world away from the humdrum realities of mundane daily life.

Part of the interior design included seventy-seven custom-made, fully functioning gas lamps. This often became a cause of concern for some of the more safety-conscious customers and employees, making people highly aware of the locations of the various fire exits.

Exterior view of the Barbary Coast, circa 1970. © *Thomas Robinson.*

To add ambiance to the interior, Dick bought a "mockup" locomotive replica from a Hollywood film studio. It consisted of a steel frame covered with wood and fiberglass. It was purchased from 20th Century Fox and had been previously used in the film *Ticket to Tomahawk* (one of Marilyn Monroe's early film credits). The replica was later used to film various scenes in the television series *Petticoat Junction*, which aired from September 1963 to April 1970. The payoff that Dick insisted on was a prominent screen credit after each episode that read, "Train furnished by Barbary Coast, Hoyt Hotel, Portland, Oregon."

There were many colorful characters from Portland and out of town who frequented the Barbary Coast at the Hoyt. Walter Cole, longtime Portlander and female impersonator better known as Darcelle, recalled the Roaring 20s Room in Sharon Knorr's book *Just Call Me Darcelle*. According to Cole, the men's restroom included a twelve-foot-long trough urinal decorated like a rock grotto, with mini forest animals that served as targets. Cole also remembered a "life-sized replica of Fidel Castro….If a gentleman could hit that open mouth, lights would flash, sirens would go off and a huge waterfall would flush the entire urinal." To add another element of grace and sophistication, there was a full-time harpist in the ladies' room playing classical music for the enjoyment of women.

The Barbary Coast restaurant and bar may also have been "the first organ equipped eatery" to open in the Pacific Northwest. In 1963, Harvey Dick purchased a 1912 Foto player organ-piano from the Arcade Theater in Hoquiam, Washington, and had it installed in the restaurant. With the organ player, a record was eventually produced that was called *Sounds of the Barbary Coast,* with Frank Elliot at the Fotoplayer and produced by Hoyt Recording Company in Portland. This LP included the tracks "Only a Bird in a Gilded Cage," "Yes, We Have No Bananas," "William Tell Overture," "I Wish I Could Shimmy Like My Sister Kate" and others.

Part of the appeal of the Barbary Coast and the Roaring 20s Room was the stylish décor. Diners were known to visit just so they could see the valuable collection of artifacts that Dick had collected and assembled over the years. The bar contained a mechanical piano and a large box filled with mechanical puppet-like musicians that would play and flop around, which customers found amusing. There was even a writing desk rumored to have belonged to Theodore Dreiser (1871–1945), a writer of the Naturalist school. Dreiser was the author of the critically acclaimed 1925 novel *An American Tragedy,* which was the first in a string of novels dealing with hyperrealism in depicting the American experience.

The Roaring 20s Room was presided over by the colorful and loquacious vaudevillian-style entertainer Gracie Hansen (1922–1985). In 1964, Dick personally invited Hansen to Portland, where he arranged for her to open the Roaring 20s Room and where she became an instant hit. Hansen was a cheerful woman, and at only five feet tall, she was a supremely confident entertainer with multiple skills.

Gracie became known for stalking out on stage and greeting the crowd by saying, "Hiya suckers!" before going into her comedic routines. Hansen was described by the Oregon Encyclopedia as being the perfect entertainer for Dick Harvey's spacious establishment: "He had seen her at the World's Fair and thought she would be 'exactly the person I need to bring entertainment to my hotel!'" A million-dollar renovation converted the hotel's five-thousand-square-foot parking garage into a five-hundred-seat dinner theater with the first hydraulic lift-stage west of the Mississippi. Hansen graced the stage until February 1971, singing and telling jokes to such personalities as Johnny Carson, John Gavin, Duke Ellington and Count Basie. The Roaring 20s Room became the premier showcase in Portland, with lines of people waiting to get in. By 1970, Hansen had written *Gracie Hansen's Horoscope for Swingers* and was reading "Horoscopes for Swingers" on KATU Channel 2's morning show.

Hansen remained Dick's most important star attraction for several years, entertaining and teasing audience members year-round. She became Dick's most valuable asset, drawing in customers nightly just to see her; she was described years later as "the one and only Gracie Hansen!"

Hansen's presence was integral to the success of the restaurant, and she well knew it. Hansen was so colorful a personality that in 1970 she ran for governor of Oregon on a "pro-entertainment platform" as a Democrat with the comical slogan "The best governor money can buy!" During the race, competing against Robert "Bob" Straub, Hansen cheerfully came in third place. After several years in Portland, however, Hansen moved in 1971 to Los Angeles to perform in clubs there and eventually to retire. She died in 1985, and in 2012, a stage play called *Gracie: A Musical Adventure* was written by Donald Horn and produced in Portland.

Scott Kruger remembered the Hoyt from the days he worked there during the summer of 1966, when he was sixteen and still in high school:

> *I worked at the Hoyt as a busboy for the restaurants—there were several, mainly I worked the Oak Room. I remember it well. When I met Gracie and the dancers, my life changed forever. A friend who ran the light show for the Roaring 20s Room would let me get into the light booth with him while he was doing the show and let me watch. What an experience, what an awakening! I fell in love with one of the dancers from an out-of-town troupe, who thought I was the cutest thing since sliced bread. She proceeded to provide a valuable education in the ways of the world. I've not been the same since—what a beautiful experience. I've cherished it all my life. Then there was Harvey Dick—what a presence, a powerful man, larger than life. I remember his Rolls Royce with the leopard interior, incredible! How lucky I was to be a part of something so special and fleeting.*

In 1972, after the departure of Gracie, Dick closed the hotel because of declining business and to make way for a bus terminal project that was ultimately built a block away instead. For nine years, the Barbary Coast at the Hoyt was the place to be seen, socialize and hook up. The Roaring 20s Room closed down only weeks before the hotel finally closed.

One longtime rumor is that Multnomah County seized the hotel for unpaid back taxes, and since the county neglected to winterize the pipes, one winter they burst on the roof and water ran through the building for several days before it was discovered. By then the waterlogged structure was essentially destroyed, and there was no option but to proceed with demolition, which occurred in 1977.

Memories of the Barbary Coast at the Hoyt are diverse and come from some surprising online sources. Harvey Dick's own grandson Stephen Chappell also remembered the Barbary Coast at the Hoyt:

> *Nice to see that my grandfather Harvey Dick and his beloved Hoyt Hotel are still remembered. My grandfather was a larger-than-life guy. I only met him once—in 1975 (he and my mom had a huge falling out when I was a baby and didn't speak for about 14 years). It was at my aunt's wedding. He brought his own special throne and sat there to receive guests. Many at the wedding had known him for decades. I'm glad I finally got to meet the man that I had heard about all my life. He passed away a little over two years later, while standing waiting for his driver.*

The Barbary Coast was a Portland jewel in the restaurant business and appealed to a variety of people from all walks of life before it shuttered. One customer of the Barbary Coast remembered his mother taking him there when he was a child. The woman was not rich and could not afford to buy a meal, but instead she would buy a coffee for herself and a glass of milk for her son. There they would sit in the Barbary Coast while his mother sipped coffee and he sipped his milk, just looking around at the beautiful décor of a lost time that had been recaptured and put on display—a portal to a glimmering and elegant past. Perhaps this is the best story to end this profile—the story of a mother and son who were both so moved by the beauty of a Portland restaurant that they went there just so they could look around and enjoy the view.

Chapter 5

Legends, Difficult Bosses, Art and a Boat

THE RIVER QUEEN, 1962–1995

The River Queen became Portland's first floating restaurant and was beloved as a place where big celebrations were possible and indeed commonplace. The vessel that became the River Queen was originally built by Bethlehem Shipbuilding in San Francisco and christened the SS *Shasta* in 1922.

As travel by car was becoming increasingly popular, the company Six Minute Ferry ordered three new steel ferries to be constructed in 1921: the SS *Shasta*, the SS *San Mateo* and the SS *Yosemite*. The Six Minute Ferry operated an automobile ferry service across Carquinez Strait, located on the main highway between Sacramento and Oakland, California. Each crossing, near the existing Interstate 80 Bridge, took about six minutes, hence the name.

In March 1922, a landslide unexpectedly destroyed the Six Minute Ferry north shore terminal on Morrow Cove. Unable to bounce back after the natural disaster and still waiting for the completion of all three vessels, the ferry company went out of business, and the three sisters were sold before being completed to Southern Pacific, taking their place in the company's already extensive fleet.

With the opening of the Bay Bridge on November 12, 1936, and the opening of the Golden Gate Bridge on May 27, 1937, the SS *Shasta* was essentially deemed unnecessary and obsolete and was put out of business. Eventually, the *Shasta*, along with its sister ship the *San Mateo*, was put up for sale and purchased by the Puget Sound Navigation Company in 1941.

Exterior photo of the River Queen. *Courtesy of Doug Roylance.*

The third ship, the *Yosemite*, had a less fortunate fate when it was purchased by the Argentina Uruguayan Navigation Company for $70,000 in 1939. The company paid Bethlehem Shipbuilding an additional $35,000 to modify the ferry to reach the Rio de la Plata on its own power: "The ferry was renamed *Argentina* and equipped with structural reinforcement, new keels, additional fuel and water tanks, a radio and quarters for a 21-man crew." The ferry saw more adventure after its expensive modifications when it sailed from San Francisco on April 16, 1940, on a nine-thousand-mile voyage led by Captain Eduardo M. Saez of the Uruguayan navy. The trip took fifty days and was presumed to be the longest for any ferry operating under its own power at that time. After working a few more years on a thirty-mile route across the Rio de la Plata, the *Argentina* was partially scrapped and converted into a barge, which sank in 1948.

The SS *San Mateo* was launched in 1922 with its sister ships, the *Shasta* and *Yosemite*, and operated as a steamship until 1940 with the Southern Pacific Golden Gate Ferries. In 1941, the *San Mateo*, after being purchased by the Puget Sound Navigation Company, operated on Puget Sound until its retirement, making its final run ("packed to her limit") from Edmonds to Kingston on Labor Day of 1969. At the time of its retirement, the *San Mateo* was the last operating vehicular steam ferry in the United States.

After attempts to restore the *San Mateo* for display in a Seattle waterfront park failed, it was purchased by a Canadian businessman who towed it to the Fraser River in British Columbia. There, it languished on the Fraser River for several years, abandoned, and was partially scrapped. Portions of its hulk are allegedly still visible in the river today. Like the SS *Shasta*, the SS *San Mateo* would eventually gain the melancholy distinction of being listed in the National Register of Historic Places for historically significant vessels and landmarks. This, despite the fact that all three sister ships, the last to be ordered constructed by the Six Minute Ferry Company, would ultimately end up abandoned, scrapped or sunk.

The SS *Shasta* in its prime was a gleaming 217-foot vessel. It operated with 1200 horsepower and could travel at a speed of thirteen knots. Powered through steam propulsion, it was considered a "smoky" vessel, which could be problematic even in those early days. It functioned for most of its early life as a ferry in the San Francisco Oakland Bay area—its name taken from the mountain of the same name located in northern California. The SS *Shasta* had room for 55 automobiles and 468 passengers and could carry a maximum tonnage of 919 tons, while traveling across the bay between San Francisco and Oakland, California. Later, on Puget Sound, the *Shasta* worked between Seattle, Bremerton, Winslow and Victoria, British Columbia. However, much like the *San Mateo*, the *Shasta* was not regularly used by the Puget Sound Navigation Company. Both ships spent much of their time in layup for a variety of maintenance reasons. Both vessels spent time working with the Black Ball Company, used as fill-in vessels when traffic was at its peak on the sound. However, by the 1940s, the *Shasta* had become seriously outdated in terms of construction, and this presented ongoing issues with its reliability as a working vessel.

Despite these problems, the *Shasta* continued to work, staying active during 1945 on the Seattle-Manchester route and in 1946 and 1947 on the Winslow-Seattle run, before being placed in layup again. By the summer of 1950, she was being put to work again as the "spare boat" on the Bremerton run. The *San Mateo* was used far more frequently and the *Shasta* less frequently, in part because the *Shasta* had a nasty habit of "belching out a significant black cloud of oil smoke from her 47-foot high smokestack." This occurred for unknown reasons but was possibly due to irregular maintenance or even faulty engineering. During the rush to complete construction of all three boats, after the Six Minute Ferry Company had gone under, it is highly possible that the building of the *Shasta* was hurried and that errors may have been made in its original construction.

The *Shasta* worked for decades as a ferry and was sold yet again in 1958 to a group of Portland businessmen who renamed the aging vessel the *Centennial Queen*. They had no real intention of keeping it long-term, and it was only used for a short while, running up and down the Columbia River as a tour

The Centennial Queen, circa 1959. *Courtesy of Doug Roylance.*

boat in honor of the Oregon Centennial Celebration of 1959 and its 100th year of statehood. Charging the outlandish (for the time) price of $2.50 for a child's ticket and $4.50 for adult tickets, which included tax, people got to tour the Willamette and Columbia Rivers and contemplate that Oregon was now 100 years old, reflecting on what that might mean.

The name change didn't alter the *Shasta*'s habit of consistently leaving a bothersome plume of black oil smoke in its wake. Even in the late 1950s, this manner of unsightly exhaust was not environmentally friendly, and the steamer was retired after the 1959 season. Ultimately, the *Centennial Queen* proved too difficult to maintain and didn't turn a profit, leaving its owners bankrupt.

But with the *Shasta*'s retirement as a troublesome working ferry behind it, the vessel would have an entirely new future. In 1962, it would change hands once more, this time purchased by Walter and Winnifred Nutting. The *Shasta* was renamed, refurbished, repainted and polished to begin its time as the gleaming and beautiful River Queen, an elegant stationary restaurant docked on the Willamette River. The River Queen became one of the city's

Top: The Centennial Queen, circa 1959. *Courtesy of Doug Roylance.*

Bottom: A River Queen advertisement. *Courtesy of Doug Roylance.*

finest steak and seafood restaurants, moored originally along the banks of the Willamette River at the Sellwood Bridge moorage. What had once been ferry seating and a snack bar were replaced with a smart-looking kitchen, a bar and a large dance floor with enough space throughout the ship to seat three hundred diners.

More excitement lay in store for the River Queen when the Christmas flood of 1964 broke the ship loose and it meandered downriver on an unfettered joyride. It had to be rescued by a bevy of local tugboats the following day, finally securing it safely at Zidell's docks. Ten days later, in early January 1965, the River Queen was taken to what would be its most permanent home, located at 1300 Northwest Front Avenue, where it was berthed. In October 1970, the River Queen was sold yet again when Harold "Bill" Roylance and his wife, Dorothy, along with Bill and Shirley Pierce, purchased the ship from its longtime owners, the Nuttings. Then, in April 1973, the short partnership dissolved, and Bill and Dorothy Roylance became the sole owners of the River Queen, a ship that was almost forty-five years old.

For more than thirty years, the River Queen operated as Portland's beloved floating restaurant, presenting its final owners a series of daunting new challenges. Operating a restaurant and maintaining a boat was more than a full-time job, and the upkeep was constant and expensive. It represented the kind of commitment only a dedicated family unit could take on. Fortunately, Bill and Dorothy Roylance were helped regularly by their four hardworking children: daughters Diana and Pam and sons Doug and Chuck. Doug Roylance remarked in an interview on the various challenges of operating a stationary restaurant, explaining bemusedly, "The River Queen was not *just* a restaurant. The River Queen was a restaurant *and* a boat!"

A River Queen employee, Barry Morris, remembered how hectic working on the River Queen could be:

> *Once, when it was a bit slow, I decided to spend some time cleaning the lounge area. The more I scrubbed it was apparent that the original paint was white, not the amber appearance that had developed with years of heavy cigarette smoking and nicotine. Mrs. Roylance, the owner, came running into the bar screaming at me to stop the scrubbing. She said that if people knew the real color of the original paint, that we'd have to scrub the entire ship and it would take forever. That same day, someone climbed to the very top of the Fremont Bridge which loomed right above us, threatening to jump. We watched as police and firemen tried to talk the guy down. After a few hours, he agreed to come down in exchange for a pizza and a pack of cigarettes.*

A band playing at the River Queen. *Courtesy of Doug Roylance.*

During the floating restaurant's heyday, the River Queen was host to many forms of entertainment, and because it was so large, the parties could get big. There were high school graduation parties, elaborate wedding receptions, birthday parties, baby showers, anniversary parties and high school prom celebrations, often with hundreds of people in attendance, sometimes even as many as 350.

The River Queen had an impressive menu with a large variety of excellent seafood with appetizers, salads, sandwiches, à la carte selections and desserts. There was the shrimp cocktail, oyster cocktail, Dungeness crab cocktail and the popular Captain's Combination Cocktail, along with the Crab Cocktail Supreme and Shrimp Cocktail Supreme. The soups were standard, with the expected soup of the day, often New England clam chowder or oyster stew. Salads were also plentiful and delicious and included the Shrimp Salad, the Royal Bengal Salad, Neptune's Tuna Delight, Chef's Gourmet Salad, Dungeness Crab Louie, Commodore's Fruit Salad and the Crab Salad, which was featured as the "Port Dock Favorite." Sandwiches on the lunch menu included the Club House, ham and turkey, a hefty reuben, the Fisherman's Special, a simple turkey and the ham on rye. It also had a Dungeness crab sandwich, along with the filet of halibut almondine, clam medallions, breaded scallops, an oyster fry, seafood fettuccini and its popular fish and chips.

Burgers included a standard hamburger, cheeseburger, bacon burger and the special Tugboat Burger, which was prepared with Swiss cheese and bleu cheese dressing on a French roll with au jus and French fries. Dinner entrées included top sirloin steak dinners, filet mignon dinner, New York strip, prime rib, scallops and stuffed or jumbo prawns, lobster dinner and Australian rock lobster tail. Desserts were simple and included French cream cheesecake, turtle cheesecake, crème de menthe mousse torte, Kahlua chocolate mousse tort, ice cream or sherbet and a strawberry or chocolate sundae.

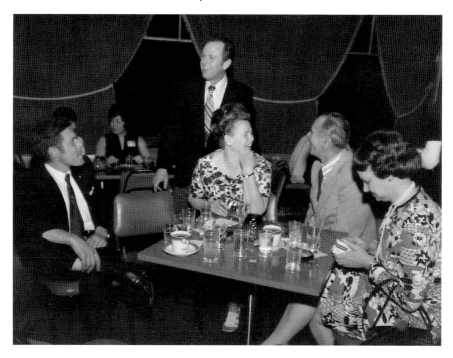

A family out enjoying the River Queen, circa 1970s. *Courtesy of Doug Roylance.*

Portlanders fondly remember the River Queen and have a nostalgic connection to the boat. Doug Crowell recalled working at the River Queen in the late 1970s and the camaraderie of one of the longtime cooks: "I loved working Sunday mornings because the opening shift cook would make us steak and eggs for breakfast on the sly." Crowell also recalled the owner's son, Doug, and how much he liked him: "I remember Doug—he was the one everyone *hoped* would be in charge during their shift. He was a really nice guy."

Crowell further shared what might happen if an employee was caught taking tips they were not entitled to:

> *I remember the owner Bill would publicly shame you if you were caught stealing tips. You'd be fired and at the time people had to pick up their paycheck in person, so if you'd been caught he would make you sit there while the other employees were picking up their checks and Bill would let them know what was going to happen. Generally, the wait staff knew what to expect tip-wise from most of the tables, so once they started coming up short, it wasn't too long before they could pinpoint who was responsible. The flip side was if they liked you, and knew you hustled, they would put in a request for you to help with larger parties and banquets to ensure the best service and therefore better tips.*

Debra Hagen Baldwin remembered the River Queen well before it shuttered: "I had my wedding reception there in 1995. There were 350 people in attendance, and the Terry Robb Trio. I was told that my wedding reception was the last big event held in the Banquet rooms."

Lois Netherton Plunkett recalled how a visit to the River Queen for lunch succeeded in inadvertently changing her life:

> *The one and only time I went there was in 1995. I was getting ready to move from the home I'd been in for twenty years to a condominium. There was a place over in Northwest where I could get boxes, and the tape was free. I didn't know the area very well, so the man I'd been dating for only a month went with me. I was still unsure of my feelings for him. He suggested we stop for lunch, and he took me to the River Queen. On that day, I learned more about him and how he had done outreach in California, where he previously lived. He helped some underprivileged kids get to a baseball game. That day I realized he was a good man. Six months later, we were married!*

A band and dancing girls, circa 1970s. *Courtesy of Doug Roylance.*

One of the reasons the River Queen was so beloved was due to the strong pull of nostalgia—the dynamic of family and friends breaking bread together. What might have been mundane experiences were made special because of the beauty of dining on what used to be a ferry. The sense of adventure and the incredible space of such a large vessel created that feeling of freedom and possibility. One Portland man, George Alderson, recalled an occasion on the River Queen and how it was the last time he saw his father before he passed away: "It was the last lunch with my father on the River Queen in the spring of 1963, just before I left town for grad school, military service and the rest of my life far from my hometown of Portland. He died a few weeks later. The River Queen was a quiet place at lunchtime on a weekday, a good place to relax and talk about my plans and his for the years ahead. I didn't know then that my parents had probably been passengers of the same boat, during the 1930s, when it was in service in San Francisco Bay and they were both college students at Berkeley."

Portland resident Ken Soesbe remembered the time spent at the River Queen and how it became an important part of his childhood memories spent with his brother:

> *My brother Tom and I grew up in Southeast Portland, and fishing was always part of our recreational activities. If we weren't fishing at Johnson Creek, near Eastmorland Park, which back in the '60s still had trout, then we would end up fishing next to the River Queen. The catch of the day there was crappie blue, gill or carp. Not for eating but just to catch and release for fun. The cooks on the River Queen would walk out to the edge of the restaurant and throw old food in the water, and the carp would come up to feed like giant goldfish. If the fishing was slow, we would walk out on the logs that were tied together waiting to be barged up the river. They were fun times back then.*

Bill Roylance had worked as a traveling distributer for Boyd's Coffee all through the 1950s and 1960s. While maintaining a friendship with Portland police officer Don DuPay's father, restaurant owner S.M. DuPay (who owned and operated DuPay's Drive-In Restaurant), Roylance would commiserate with S.M. during his monthly visits to drop off Boyd's Coffee at DuPay's. Roylance would question S.M. about the specifics of operating a restaurant, and they would talk for hours about his dream of one day opening up his own place. Roylance certainly got his wish with the River Queen, as it presented one of the biggest challenges of his life. It was Roylance who had been the biggest promoter of the River Queen, maintaining a long and complex connection to the old ferry and continuing with the restaurant when others might have not seen the benefits for doing so.

The River Queen presented constant maintenance problems, and to completely restore it would have required several million dollars. It was fixed as problems presented themselves, but because of the expense, a complete overhaul was regularly put off. In 1995, Bill Roylance became ill, and then around the same time, the River Queen lost its moorage. So, it was announced that it would be shuttered. On the register for historical vessels and landmarks, the River Queen's real name was still listed as the SS *Shasta*.

Doug Roylance remembered the lengths his father went to care for the aging boat and maintain it, mostly because of his father's dedication to the vessel and his strong desire to see it maintained and saved. It's hard not to wonder if perhaps Bill Roylance didn't in some way personify the old boat, as his preoccupation with its fate is noteworthy in the family's recollections of his dedication to the old ferry.

It was a melancholy day for Portland when it was publicly announced that the River Queen would shutter. Because business had been slowing down, with the introduction of new restaurants all over Portland, sometimes there was only a skeleton crew working. Juli Norman, a longtime employee, remembered working at the River Queen. She also remembered the crazy last few days after Bill Roylance announced that the River Queen would be closing:

> *I remember a lot of blue shenanigans going on. One memory I can share is the Saturday after Mr. Roylance, who we all called Mr. R, announced on the local news that the River Queen was closing for good. There were only three of us working that day, and within minutes of opening we were completely full. Business had dwindled on the weekends, so we had a skeleton crew. No bartender, only one chef and two servers. I was one of the servers, and I doubled as the bartender. Mr. Liggins, who was the chef, could only do so much. Alcohol was keeping most people happy, and I got to hear bits and pieces of the memories being reminisced. The dining room that day was filled with business attire, formal attire, jeans, down to mariners shorts and flip flops. Sea lions were cruising by on their way to the falls in Oregon City, grain ships turning around with the assistance of two tugboats and coming very close to the diners. I will never forget the best job I ever had!*

Part of the powerful appeal of the River Queen was due to the vast expanse of the vessel, the gorgeous views and the feeling of happiness and excitement that amount of free space gives people. The floating restaurant would gently move with the tides as it rested on the Willamette, particularly if a barge passed by, and it was that rocking motion that was so restful and memorable. Cori-Ann Woodward recalled how comforting that was: "I loved the slow back and forth of the tides of the Willamette River, elbowing the edges of the ship as we ate our food."

After the River Queen was shuttered and sat on the water for many years, the forlorn old ferry was moved yet again to the Columbia River between Deer Island and Goble, Oregon, just off Highway 30. A man named Clay Jonak purchased the old boat and leased the site near Goble in 2012 in the hopes of finally restoring the old River Queen. However, the site ended up merely becoming a collector's nightmare where derelict boats were gathered and purchased cheaply so they might be restored. That generally did not happen with most of the boats. City officials claim that Jonak brought in two dozen boats over the years, neglected them and in fact did nothing to restore them. Three of the large boats ended up sinking, becoming a clear danger to the health of the river and the natural environment.

The River Queen spent years slowly deteriorating in the unforgiving elements, and when news footage began circulating detailing the imminent danger it was in, numerous websites sprang up with concerns over its fate. The websites shared fond references to "the old gal" and "the grand lady" and how much it had meant to Portlanders for one sentimental reason or another.

On one website, Michael Beardsley fervently asked for the public's help: "Tug boats are not secured cheaply. All that said I believe that she deserves better than the scrapper's torch and I know that someone with passion and effort could do something great with her. She is on the historic register, and that mostly governs her exterior appearance, one could do whatever they wanted to for the interior. She really will go to the first person who puts up their hand and says, 'I'll take her.'"

Sadly, no one was interested in spending a small fortune restoring the grand lady, and it was left alone to the elements and the damage of time and continued indifference. The years went by, and the seasons with their brutal cold and relentless heat wreaked their neutral and unequivocal havoc on the old boat. The River Queen was, of course, vandalized repeatedly, and most of the lovely old fittings that held any value were pulled up, torn off and taken away by thieves and drug addicts. It decayed more each year, and eventually the roof began collapsing in sections, destroying much of the once beautiful stained-glass windows. The city was notified and then the Coast Guard. The Coast Guard believed—and rightly so—that the boat presented enough of a present danger that it declared the site and the abandoned ferry to be a serious hazard. It was ordered to be scrapped by the USCG, and the process was begun in the summer of 2018.

By July of that year, the River Queen had been stripped to the hull. The life of the beautiful ferry, the longest lived of the three sister ships, was ended. With nearly a full century of varied history connected to the once elegant San Francisco Bay steamer, time during which it affected the lives of countless people, the River Queen (or, as it was still legally named, the SS *Shasta*) continues to remain unforgettable. For a stationary vessel, it provided thousands of Portlanders and others with adventure, laughter and wonder, and it became both the destination and the journey.

DER RHEINLÄNDER RESTAURANT, 1963–2016

Der Rheinländer Restaurant, formerly located at 5053 Northeast Sandy Boulevard, opened its doors at a time when there weren't many German restaurants in Portland. A Portland website fondly remembered Der Rheinländer: "Founded in 1963 by chef Horst Mager, a German immigrant from Wiesbaden Germany, it was a loved jewel box of stuccoed walls, timbered woods, cuckoo clocks, and many imported German decorations."

Der Rheinländer went from a leased space seating 60 people, to 80 people and then 130 people. In time, the expanded restaurant, taking up almost a full city block, could accommodate up to 300 hungry customers.

Horst Mager was an ebullient force in Portland's restaurant world. He was a true character with a thick German accent who loved to cheerfully advise people that Rheinländer's "shicken dinner" was one of its most popular. In terms of misconceptions about German cuisine, Mager was quoted as saying, "German food is incorrectly considered 'heavy.' Actually it uses lean meat, vegetables, little oil and has fewer calories than Italian or Mexican."

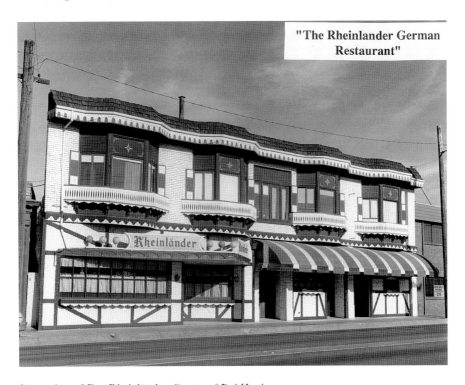

Street view of Der Rheinländer. *Courtesy of Joel Hamberg.*

A very young Horst Mager.
Courtesy of Joel Hamberg.

Horst Mager and staff. *Courtesy of Joel Hamberg.*

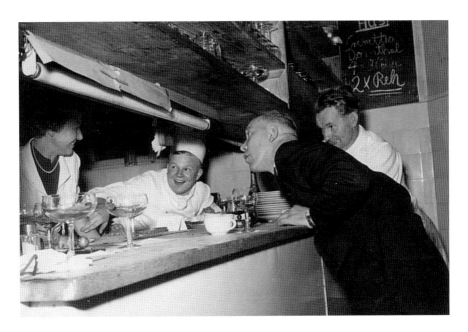

Early shot of a playful Horst Mager while still in Germany. *Courtesy of Joel Hamberg.*

In terms of popularity and overall influence, Mager was probably only second to Henry Thiele. However, Mager was a star, a true Portland original and a showman. Much of Portland must have looked on Horst Mager as the second coming of James Beard, who was a true cuisinier and a legend in his own right.

Mager came to the United States in the 1950s, having been raised in the restaurant business with his father, who was also a chef, with Mager arriving in Portland in 1959. He learned the tricks of the trade, benefiting from the European apprenticeship system and from his father, who operated a restaurant in Hesse, Germany. His father's restaurant provided the hearty, traditional German fare that people wanted. After coming to the States and visiting a sister in Missouri, Mager decided that he would begin working in the business he knew so well and took a job at the Sheraton Hotel in St. Louis. Celebrated Portland author Heather Arndt Anderson recounted Mager's steady rise to prominence:

In 1959, when the Lloyd Center shopping mall was being built, Sheraton recruited the 28-year-old to come to Oregon and open the restaurant in its new Portland hotel, the Lloyd Center Sheraton. After proving his mettle as a sous chef in a first-class hotel kitchen, Mager bought into widow Maria

Kald's restaurant, Maria's Swedish Dinners on Northeast Sandy Boulevard, and took over as head chef in 1963. At Maria's, Mager was able to relax a bit from stuffy hotel fare and cook the food of the Fatherland—family specialties that came naturally to the seventh-generation chef. His ascent was celestial. In 1964, he was selected for a Chef's Choice award by the Chefs du Cuisine Society of Oregon. The following year, Mager changed the name of the restaurant to the one it bears today—Der Rheinländer— and the television offers began to roll in.

Kerry-Lynne Brown also remembered the transition from Maria's Swedish Dinners to Der Rheinländer and how it evolved from one restaurant into another: "Before it was the Rheinländer's, it was Maria's Swedish Dinners, owned and operated by Mrs. Maria Kald. They cooked a lot of Scandinavian-type dishes. My Swedish grandmother cooked and served at the restaurant and lived across the street in the big old house that once stood where the barbershop now stands. My mother used to go and sit in the back of the restaurant while my grandmother worked. Maria hired Horst, and he eventually bought out Maria and then built it into the Rheinländer."

In 1965, Mager, described by more than one former employee as a bit of a "tyrant," would begin appearing on a Portland cooking show called *Chef's Gourmet* on KOIN-TV, showing Portlanders how to make simple German dishes. Throughout the 1960s and early 1970s, he became a regular of the program and would become a Portland celebrity in his own right before eventually becoming the show's host in 1973.

In many respects, Horst became the local equivalent of Julia Child and Graham Kerr. He then began appearing on another TV cooking show, called *KOIN Kitchen*. What had once been, with Lois Devore, a program devoted to good, simple family fare on a budget, became a platform for a larger-than-life German man who enjoyed an audience and holding court among his admirers and fans.

Mager, through his company, Specialty Restaurants, opened several restaurants over the years; however, most of them did not take off. This included Blarney's Castle, which had an Irish motif; Chateau La France, with a French motif; and the Couch Street Fish House, located in Old Town, which was quite popular for a time. Couch Street Fish House opened in October 1976 and served dishes like smoked beluga sturgeon, iced cherrystone clams, oysters Rockefeller and Belgian endive with lemon and cream dressing.

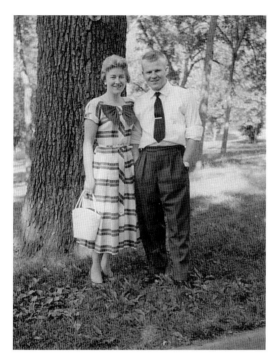

Left: An early shot of Horst Mager. *Courtesy of Joel Hamberg.*

Below: Portland mayor Frank Ivancie at Der Rheinländer, circa 1975. *Courtesy of Joel Hamberg.*

Master Chef Horst Mager

Above: Horst Mager cooking for the camera. *Courtesy of Joel Hamberg.*

Left: Horst Mager filming his cooking show. *Courtesy of Joel Hamberg.*

Opposite: Horst Mager in publicity still. *Courtesy of Joel Hamberg.*

Worth mentioning is Mager's other restaurant, L'Omelette, which featured an open kitchen and proved to be a resounding success, becoming popular with James Beard and Julia Child. L'Omelette continually pushed Portland toward a new level of sophistication and away from the commonly perceived provincialism Portland was known for due to its less celebrated eating establishments.

Naturally, Der Rheinländer was a popular location with families, who wanted to celebrate birthday parties, high school graduations, wedding receptions and anniversary parties there. Portland grade schools and high schools promoted learning about German cuisine, and their history and language study groups arranged regular evening field trips to the restaurant. Charles Rynerson remembered going to Der Rheinländer for a school outing: "It was an annual thing for my German classes in the late 1970s. It wasn't really a field trip. It was an evening thing, which was not a problem because we all lived in Northeast, and high school students in the 1970s didn't need their parents to chaperone them. We were required to speak German while there, and it would have been my first time trying fondue. *That* was probably the best part of the experience."

The restaurant was not only loved because of its great German food but also because, in many ways, it acted as a kind of local playground for children and young people, as Matthew Korfhage of the *Willamette Week* described: "Der Rheinländer has always been as much a theme park as restaurant—a castle and patio with countless rooms filled with knick-knacks and echt-Deutscher kitsch."

Some of the tasty appetizers included the fondue sampler and the basil pesto fondue, as well as the Bavarian pretzels served with fondue and bread. There was the crab and roasted red pepper fondue, served with grilled crusty bread; the smoked bier sausage, served with fondue and cubed bread (gluten-free upon request); and the Swiss cheese fondue.

The meat and fish dishes were delicious and versatile, featuring savory roast pork with apricot-cherry chutney, German cabbage rolls, shepherd's pie, roast turkey breast, fish and chips and German meatballs with fresh caper sauce. There was the bratwurst, bier and weisswurt sausages, pan-sautéed Pacific Northwest salmon, charbroiled trout, charbroiled chicken

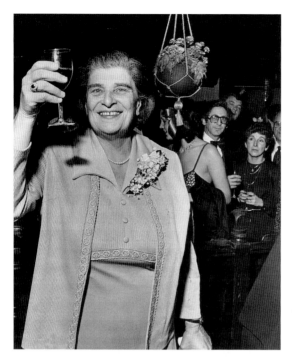

Left: Mildred Schwab making a toast, circa 1975. *Courtesy of Joel Hamberg.*

Below: A full restaurant. *Courtesy of Joel Hamberg.*

breast, lamb shank, braised pork knuckle with horseradish sauce, pork cordon bleu and flat-iron steak, all of which were served daily.

Der Rheinländer had what it called the family "feasts" for larger groups to share. These included the Rheinländer Feast—sauerbraten, pork schnitzel cordon bleu and smoked bier sausage with caramelized onions, served with spätzle noodles, braised red cabbage and sauerkraut. There was the Munich Feast, comprising veal jagerschnitzel with sautéed mushrooms in a creamy paprika sauce. The menu also featured pork schnitzel cordon bleu with lemon wedges, served with spätzle noodles, braised red cabbage, sauerkraut and an oven-baked Bavarian-style pretzel with an assortment of tangy mustards. Other dishes included German potato pancakes and grilled bratwurst. Popular sandwiches included Gustav's Grilled Rueben, the French dip, roast pork sandwich, the Schnitzel Club, the grilled cheese and onion and the robust roast turkey sandwich.

Desserts included chocolate brownies, which could be served with vanilla ice cream or whipped cream; chocolate mousse in a Florentine shell, which came with a hint of brandy; and the famous Bavarian crème, served with a raspberry puree. The apple strudel was another popular dessert, served with raisins and sweet spices, glazed with apricot jam and dusted with powdered confectioners' sugar. There was the dense chocolate lovers' flourless cake, with bittersweet chocolate, spiked with Kahlua, topped with tiny bits of toffee and served with a whiskey caramel sauce and fresh whipped cream. Should those desserts somehow fail to be tempting, there was Gustav's beloved Old Fashioned Bread Pudding and, of course, its famous crème brulée, a succulent vanilla custard that was baked and then topped with caramelized sugar.

Despite Der Rheinländer's large menu and delicious food, it was not without the occasional misstep. One customer, Emily Othus, recalled during a visit in 1978 that she felt a soft, funny sensation near her ankle and wondered what it was. "I felt a furry thing around my feet and I looked down, and it was *not* a kitty. It was a dying rat having a seizure. When I summoned the waiter, he remarked, 'Yeah, we have rats here.'"

Gena Fields remembered that Der Rheinländer's was "the best place to go for underage drinking during the 1990s. They even served my friend's little sister who was only fifteen at the time!"

Mike Lindberg, a retired Portland city commissioner, remembered a trip to Rheinländer's and that the wine was not the best quality, which was unusual given Horst Mager's immense knowledge of fine wine. This resulted in a funny situation later as Lindberg and his friend and their wives were

A young Horst Mager serving guests, including Mark Hatfield. *Courtesy of Joel Hamberg.*

getting into their cars and saying goodnight: "If you bought a complete dinner, they provided a large carafe of white wine. I had a difficult boss in my job in a corporation at the time. He suggested dinner with our wives at Rheinländer's. Everything was jolly with the four of us until the dinner was over. Then my boss became sick in the parking lot. Horst Mager was a celebrity in his own right, though. He cooked on the *AM Northwest* TV show with Jim Bosley."

Horst Mager could be a harsh taskmaster at times, like many motivated restaurant owners. Darlene Richardson remembered an incident that happened in 1998 when the executive chef position was given to a woman named Robin Flower: "Robin held that position until about 2010. Robin told me a story about some kid who was working in the restaurant and broke a bunch of dishes accidentally. Horst demanded that the kid hand over his watch, and when he did, Horst put the watch on the floor. He threatened to crush it under his foot, screaming at the kid about how those dishes belonged to *him* and since the kid broke his belongings, *he* should destroy the watch." Mager did not destroy the watch.

Mager could also be quite creative. During the early years of Der Rheinländer's existence, the legal purchases of supplies could become

Horst Mager at work. *Courtesy of Joel Hamberg.*

problematic. Former detective Don DuPay of the Portland Police Bureau remembered one memorable incident in the late 1960s involving Horst Mager. After arresting an employee of a high-end seafood supply house located in downtown's Old Town, DuPay learned that the man in question had been delivering cases of expensive frozen lobster to a well-known Portland restaurant—stolen lobster, that is!

DuPay was able, however, to nip the illegal activity in the bud. It hadn't been going on very long because the seafood suppliers spotted the discrepancy in their inventory and contacted the Portland police in a timely manner. The suppliers, two men in their forties, were justifiably angry when they discovered their product disappearing, and they wanted answers. DuPay remembered walking into a chilly air-conditioned building that "reeked of raw fish and other seafood" on a warm summer day when he would rather have been anywhere else but there. When DuPay met with the owners of the supply store, they spoke quietly with him for several minutes, explaining what they had observed over the span of a few weeks and who they suspected of the theft.

They pointed out who they believed was stealing the lobster. From across the large room, DuPay saw a young Mexican man working in the far end of the building loading boxes of seafood into a truck. After a few minutes, the owners brought the young man into a back office, and DuPay questioned him in the presence of the two owners: "I remember the kid was a young wiry man, kind of muscular with perfect white teeth and jet black hair. The kind of guy you could tell was used to hard work. I leaned on him a little bit when he became evasive and uncooperative, convincing him it was in *his* best interest to tell me the truth."

DuPay continued: "At one point, I told him, 'We know you've been stealin' seafood. Now, I wanna know *where* you've been sellin' it!' The young man caved instantly and confessed that he had been delivering stolen frozen lobster to Horst Mager, for half its actual worth, *and* that he had been paid in cash by Mager himself." This new information was tantalizing for Detective DuPay, who was well aware of Mager and who he was. DuPay wanted to interview Mager personally, so he booked the young man into the jail for theft and then drove directly across town to speak with Horst in the flesh:

I walked in and after introducing myself to a passing waiter, I requested to speak with Horst. I was escorted to his office in the back, where I introduced myself to Mr. Mager as Detective DuPay with the Portland Police. I told him flat out that I was investigating the theft of stolen lobster from Pacific Seafood and that he had been buying it. Mager was surprised to see me, a police detective standing in front of him. He pushed back in his chair, a grim look on his face as I leaned over his desk. I didn't give him the opportunity to think I'd believe any lies. I told him I knew he'd been buying stolen lobster and not to waste my time denying it. When he asked how I knew that, I told him the name of the young Mexican man who I had arrested less than an hour before. As soon as I told him the name, Mager's face fell and he sighed. Mager was used to bossing people around and now the shoe was on the other foot. I asked him: "Do you wanna take delivery on that next crate of lobster and join the Mexican kid in jail?" He decided he didn't want any part of that.

At the conclusion of the interview, Mager seemed to understand what was at stake if he continued to purchase black market lobsters, and he agreed that he would no longer bend the rules. DuPay concluded with this recollection:

Mager was silent for a minute. He seemed embarrassed. I knew this was probably not something he was used to. I waited for him to respond, and he admitted he was not interested in anymore black market lobster. At the time, I was working on an important burglary case, and though I wanted to interview Mager personally, just for the novelty of saying I had, and even after giving the guy a stern warning, I was tired and disgusted. I didn't want to come back out and deal with him again. As I stood in front of his desk, I told him, "I don't wanna hear about this kinda crap happening anymore!" Without responding to my remark, Mager nodded in agreement, and I turned on my heel and left. I knew I'd made my point.

Some of the staff, including one of the well-known accordion players, Victor Meindl, were regularly decked out in bundhosen and Tyrole hats. Victor was generally occupied playing the birthday polka song, the anniversary waltz or "Auf Wiedersehen" and could still be a bit traditional about the ways that Portland was changing. This included the ways that people were welcoming diversity and equality to all people, including gay and lesbian folks. Sandra Hetzel remembered a festive celebration with friends and family after she and her wife were married: "My wife and I reserved a room for a dinner party with family the weekend of our wedding. When the server came in to sing to us, he understood that it was for a couple of brides. The accordion player had not figured that out. The look on his face when I sat on my wife's lap during the song was priceless."

Tom Shrader, a former employee of Der Rheinländer, remembered some of the drama that went on behind the scenes, common for a busy and popular restaurant with a large wait staff:

I worked there from 1969 to 1971. My favorite story took place in the summer of 1970. Horst had just gotten a new Jaguar XK 12 from Monte Shelton. It was a white convertible. He also had a new girlfriend who was a waitress at the restaurant. Apparently she had a boyfriend who was not too fond of Horst. One night, Horst went to start his Jaguar, and it wouldn't start because someone had put sugar in the gas tank. The Jaguar and his relationship to the waitress didn't last long. I recall the waitress's name was "Bridget," and she was about four inches taller than Horst. They made an interesting pair.

Some Portlanders' memories of Der Rheinländer are more traditionally sentimental. Portlander Alex McNabb remembered going to Rheinländer as a child and how enchanting it was for her:

As a young child, my parents would take me there. I couldn't understand how it was a restaurant. Going through the rooms, I thought I had been taken to a different country called "Germany." I wanted to explore all the rooms. The endless array of things to look at, the smells I had never smelled before, the accordion music and singers of strange songs. I truly was transported to a land I had never seen. The most memorable time in my teen years was a date. He was my summer of 1984 boyfriend. He asked me where I wanted to go, and I told him Rheinländer's. We got dressed up and enjoyed a splendid meal. When the check came, he turned white and got flustered. He took out his wallet and counted his bills. I asked what was wrong. He told me he didn't have enough to pay for it. He told the waitress his dilemma, and she laughed and said, "Well, looks like you'll be in the kitchen doing some dishes!" When she saw how utterly defeated and embarrassed he was, she took him to the front desk telephone so he could call his father. Dad came to the rescue and got him the rest of the cash. But to his credit, he never once asked if I had any money to cover it. Rheinländer is forever etched in my memories.

Jeff Velasco remembered dining at Rheinländer's in the 1970s with his grandmother and brother. Living as they did around the corner from the restaurant, they were able to visit often. He also remembered being hired to sweep the sidewalk in the front as a small boy and how grateful he felt for the opportunity to make a little pocket money:

I used to sweep the sidewalk once a week for one dollar-a-go. I was about eleven or twelve. I swept up most of the block, including in front of other businesses. I'd start with a push broom and sweep up any gravel or cigarette butts, then sweep up the pile into a dust pan and put it in the garbage. I'd sweep past Pat's Tavern to the Der Rheinländer. I would sweep the front of the Rheinländer, and the parking lot. Horst Mager himself would pay me out of his own pocket. Then I'd go across the street on Sandy Boulevard to the Douglas Gas Station, which is a hair salon now, and sweep the lot for Jody, the owner of the station. Then I'd go to Ray's U-Haul. Ray's was worth a dollar and a free Coke. I usually came home at the end of the day with five bucks. That was a lot of money in 1968 and 1969 for a little kid. When I was young, my parents didn't have a lot of money. A lot of the kids in the neighborhood were in the same boat. We had to figure out honest ways to make our spending money. Basically we had to work for it. It taught us the value of money and how hard it was to come by.

As Mager got older, he tired of the frantic pace of restaurant work and decided to open his own culinary school where he could pass on the countless things he'd learned about German cuisine over the decades. Heather Arndt Anderson of Eater Portland, Oregon noted, "The Horst Mager Culinary Institute opened in the Olds, Wortman and King department store building on Southwest Tenth and Alder in 1983 (later to be renamed Western Culinary Institute, now Le Cordon Bleu College of Culinary Arts). Mager also had a series of endorsement deals; Reser's Fine Foods gave him his own line of Bavarian potato salads."

After years of creating the best German food in Portland and maintaining a thriving business, Mager gave over the work of running the restaurant to his daughter Suzeanne. For many years, she handled the restaurant, and the popularity of the restaurant was unchanged. In due time, however, Der

Rheinländer chose to close its doors. This was a sad time for Portlanders who had loved their special visits to the restaurant, the excellent German food and the wonderful ambiance, as well as the festive German music.

Shuttering the beloved restaurant was not an easy choice to make, according to Suzeanne: "This decision didn't happen overnight; we've been discussing it for a long time. I have bittersweet feelings about it of course. But I feel it's the right thing to do, especially considering today's Portland food scene. It has been evolving, and so must we." Suzeanne went on to lament, "We have hosted three—and in some cases four—generations of customers at Der Rheinländer. A number of our employees met their spouses here, started families of their own and later some of their children grew up to work in the restaurant themselves. We've hosted engagements, rehearsal dinners, receptions, anniversaries, wakes, memorials and provided a venue for holiday parties and celebrations of all kinds—many important milestones and significant life events."

After some confusion regarding what would occupy the space that Der Rheinländer had occupied, a much-needed Portland Clinic took over the spot that was once one of Portland's most beloved German restaurants. The building was eventually demolished and a new clinic built in its place, with enough space for forty-five parking spaces.

Many Portlanders were bitterly unhappy with the restaurant shuttering and the demolition of the whimsical old building. "Enjoying dinners at the Rheinländer has been as much a part of our family as any other Portland tradition," said Dick Clark, the Portland Clinic CEO. "While we were very sad to hear that the Rheinländer is closing its doors, we take solace in knowing that the space will be used to continue to serve the city in a positive way. As one of this city's oldest medical practices we take pride in our deep historic Portland roots and want to continue to serve as part of the fabric of this beautiful region."

Der Rheinländer will be always be known and remembered as a festive and happy place in which entire families enjoyed the highest-quality German cuisine available. It will remain one of Portland's unforgettable eating establishments, secure in the city's collective memory, much like the colorful and cheerful German Horst Mager, who created Der Rheinländer and made his restaurant legendary in the Portland restaurant scene.

Among its many memorable offerings, Rheinländer's lentil soup was extremely popular.

Horst Mager's Lentil Soup

INGREDIENTS
¾ cup diced carrots
¾ cup diced celery
¾ cup diced onions
6 tablespoons of vegetable oil
3 ounces diced bacon
¾ cup of flour
14 cups of water
¼ cup bouillon granules
1 cup lentils
1 teaspoon salt
2 bay leaves
Pinch nutmeg
Pinch white pepper

DIRECTIONS
Sauté carrots, celery and onions in oil. Sauté bacon in a large pan. Combine and add flour, stirring constantly. Slowly add water. Add remaining ingredients and simmer about 3 hours.

• • • •

This is the famous and traditional fondue recipe that chef Horst Mager created himself. He would sometimes sell the recipe to interested customers. This recipe was shared by Sue Nevitt, who watched Horst Mager sell the recipe to her mother in the summer of 1969 for fifty cents, written down on a scrap of paper.

Horst Mager's Cheese Fondue

INGREDIENTS
2 cups white Sauterne
1 cup boiling water
1 teaspoon butter or margarine
2 pounds Darigold Swiss American cheese, cut into 1-inch cubes

½ teaspoon garlic salt
¼ teaspoon seasoned salt
¼ teaspoon salt
3 teaspoons cornstarch

DIRECTIONS
Bring the wine, water and butter to a soft boil in the double boiler. Add the cheese cubes to the wine mixture several pieces at a time, stirring constantly with a wooden spoon until melted. Continue to stir for several minutes; soon you'll see the cheese become thick and ropey. It will scorch if you don't constantly stir. This can take 20 minutes or so. After the cheese is melted, add the salts. You can add the cornstarch in a bit of water, adding it later if needed to add thickness. Serve with chunks of pumpernickel, rye bread, French bread, thick pretzels, breadsticks or German sausage—even veggies and fruit. If Darigold is unavailable in your areas, you can buy 2 pounds of white American cheese.

• • • •

OLD WIVES' TALES RESTAURANT, 1980–2014

For more than thirty-four years, the iconic Old Wives' Tales restaurant, owned and operated by attorney Holly Hart, was a welcoming place for vegetarians, vegans and those with gluten allergies and other food sensitivities. With the 90 percent gluten-free menu, those with gluten intolerance could come to the Old Wives' Tales and select from a menu of delicious dishes; it was a place where their food allergies would be taken seriously.

Hart felt that it was important to consider the needs of her customer base because she knew that food allergies could be serious: "Nobody talked about gluten intolerance, but they'd come in and say: 'I can't eat wheat.' Sometimes they wouldn't want sugar in their dessert or couldn't eat cabbage. I became aware that people have special dietary needs."

Rachel Clark, daughter of twice-elected Portland mayor Bud Clark, remembered the Old Wives' Tales and what it meant to her: "I became a vegetarian in 1986 and continued with it for eighteen years. Later, I

Exterior view of the front of the restaurant. *Courtesy of photographer Scott Allen Tice.*

became an omnivore again, but for a long time the Old Wives' Tales was one of the only places with a good and wide selection of healthier vegetarian food—and not just pasta and iceberg lettuce salads, which you could find anywhere."

All were welcome to visit and enjoy the quality food. Ray Davies of The Kinks bragged to his friends that he visited the restaurant each time he came to Portland. The British singer Boy George was seen eating at the Old Wives' Tales, as were many other celebrities, politicians and actors.

The Old Wives' Tales first opened in 1980 as a multi-ethnic vegetarian, chicken and seafood restaurant serving foods from around the world. It became a hub for feminists, gay rights activists and environmental activists. The restaurant became known as a place where enlightened, like-minded individuals with a passion for social justice, progressive politics and great food could come together, socialize, problem solve and make plans for the future.

Located at 1300 East Burnside Street, the Old Wives' Tales was formerly a pizza parlor called The Keg, which had been popular during the 1970s. With an impressive 4,455 square feet, the restaurant encompassed three separate areas in which to dine, including a room called the Classical Music Room near the back southern-facing portion of the building.

Sunlight poured in from windows on the north and west sides of the sturdy-looking 1931 structure. This created a bright, cheerful atmosphere for the spacious booths situated next to the windows. With thriving potted plants placed next to the windows and intricate decorative quilts of colorful fabrics adorning the walls, customers enjoyed a pleasant, homey ambiance. Then there was the benefit of a selection of community resource guides and newspapers, including the *Portland Tribune* and the *Oregonian*, among others, next to the front door.

There was a popular kids menu and a secure playroom north of the kitchen area, replete with mirrors and a hutch. Hart remembered the play structure well: "There were steps so that children could climb into the play structure, which was a 'Freedom Train' with a Rastafarian locomotive engineer." The playroom was a huge draw for small children and toddlers, especially on the weekend. The playroom allowed parents a chance to enjoy their food, knowing that their children were safe, entertained and always visible.

Originally from Chicago, owner Holly Hart came of age in a Jewish neighborhood, coming to Portland in 1964 to attend Reed College, where she was an international studies major and volunteered regularly with civil rights and anti-war groups. In 1969, Hart changed her focus and became more involved with fighting for gay rights and women's liberation, striving particularly for equal rights for women.

Before Hart graduated from Reed College, she'd been writing feminist articles for the *Willamette Bridge* in 1970 when her co-staff member John Wilkinson proposed the formation of a group called the Portland Gay Liberation Front. It was during this time that Hart finally chose to come out as gay. She offered her political organizing experience to help Wilkinson and his partner, Dave Davenport, launch Oregon's first politically oriented lesbian and gay male organization. The group acted as "a social and political action group for lesbians and gay men" during a pivotal time in Portland history.

Hart wrote countless *Willamette Bridge* articles encouraging gay people to come out, stop hiding and claim their place in Portland and the world. Hart also wrote articles and commentaries under pseudonyms so other gay women wouldn't think that she was the only lesbian in Portland with the courage to do so. In doing this, Hart was encouraging other gay women to speak out and claim their voice. By writing articles with the message

Photo of the playroom structure, which was popular with children and parents. *Courtesy of photographer Scott Allen Tice.*

that it was okay to be gay, Hart directly changed the culture of Portland in a meaningful and substantive way. Hart had a direct impact on how the mainstream of society perceived being gay, making it more acceptable, less hidden and less fraught with shame and secrecy.

In time, Hart became a lawyer, leaving Portland to study at the University of California–Berkeley law school. Upon returning to Portland in 1975, Hart served as chairperson on the Oregon Task Force on Sexual Preference from 1976 to 1978. Although she never actually met or worked with the Oregon governor Robert "Bob" Straub, she was appointed directly by him to be the chairperson while he was governor.

When Hart wasn't working in those early days, she was contemplating her longtime dream of opening a bookstore as a resource center and gathering place for women. That ambition morphed over time due to the complex needs and desires of many of her close friends, and the bookstore eventually became a restaurant. Hart felt that her restaurant was a needed alternative to bars or taverns, with their requisite alcohol and cigarette sales and the poor health and bad behavior that sometimes accompany those vices.

Hart recalled, "Old Wives' Tales was originally intended to be a feminist restaurant, bookstore and feminist community center. Due to limited capital, I started with restaurant service with the plan to install the bookstore after the restaurant was up and running. For various reasons, I was not able to add the bookstore. I wanted Portland to have a feminist restaurant and bookstore because other large cities already had them. Up until that time, the only gathering spaces for gays and lesbians were bars. They were alcohol based. As someone who doesn't drink, I wanted to provide an alternative to that."

It was important that the restaurant become more than a restaurant only for women, as Hart explained: "Gay men started coming to OWT because I reached out to them that they would be welcome. It quickly became a gathering place for gay men as well as lesbians because it offered an alternative for people who were too young to get into bars and for people who wanted alternatives to socializing around the consumption of alcohol."

Hart's Jewish heritage is also important, and she shared that focus with the Jewish community in Portland while running her restaurant. Hart regularly hosted a get-together for Jewish folks living on Portland's eastside and was remembered as saying, "I was looking for lost tribes."

In time, Hart would move to Hillsdale to be closer to the Mittleman Jewish Community Center and Congregation of Neveh Shalom. Being so involved in the Jewish community, Hart was dedicated to community food donations, making certain the surplus restaurant food was never wasted: "If I could, I'd spend all day preparing food to send out to the community. I personally do that—it's not just leftovers. We donate on a regular monthly basis and support a variety of organizations—feminists, street kids, refugees. This gets back to why I started the restaurant. We support the *missions* of these organizations."

Interior view of the restaurant, with coffee. *Courtesy of photographer Scott Allen Tice.*

Dishes included were those of the Greek tradition, Indian, Italian and Southeast Asian. There were plenty of chicken and seafood dishes, including a hearty turkey sandwich

A photo of some delicious butternut squash soup. *Courtesy of photographer Scott Allen Tice.*

Interior view of a table with menus and water. *Courtesy of photographer Scott Allen Tice.*

and a guacamole sandwich with bay shrimp, along with a chicken sausage sandwich on gluten-free bread. The top-notch salad bar—with its extensive selection of chopped vegetables, various lettuces, herbs, pasta, nuts, fruit and the delicious in-house dressings—was known throughout the city as one of the best. It had a transparent plastic "sneeze guard" that protected the contents from ill customers or any possible contamination. The equally famous soups, specifically the Hungarian Mushroom Soup, rich with sour cream, were daily favorites, along with the hearty lentil, minestrone and a rich butternut squash soup. The soups and salads were so popular that customers often returned for the soup and the salad bar alone.

There was the turkey frank hotdog, popular with kids, the cornmeal pancake and a poppy seed pancake served with marionberry compote and real whipped cream, which could be ordered whole or half for children or adults. A favorite breakfast item was the East Indian Rancheros. It was a generously portioned dish with enough left over to take home and create another meal. Typical huevos rancheros comprises corn tortillas, eggs and refried beans. The East Indian version made at the Old Wives' Tales replaced the refried beans with red lentil tomato dal, which is a traditional Indian dish and typically served with Indian bread and basmati rice. The salsa was replaced with pineapple-apple chutney. Another favorite on the lunch and dinner menu was the ling cod piccata, served with fresh quinoa pilaf.

A popular breakfast or middle-of-the-day snack item was the Moroccan oatmeal. The oats were rolled rather than steel cut, and it was served with raisins, apricots, dates, coriander, cinnamon, turmeric, milk or cream and either brown sugar or maple syrup. There was also the popular Greek omelet, served with mushrooms, fresh onion, tomato, feta cheese, sweet peppers, Greek olives, garlic and an assortment of fresh herbs. There was the Greek sandwich and an assortment of tofu scrambles, along with "sesame sweet potato mash made with luscious sesame oil," as Hart remembered it. There was a traditional grilled cheese sandwich and excellent rosemary chicken sandwiches along with gluten-free salmon cakes.

Desserts included cheesecake, a rich frosted chocolate cake and carob mousse, which were hits with kids. There was chocolate mousse, lemon mousse and a light, delicious raspberry mousse. There was the Apple Dutch Baby and, of course, the vegan oatmeal cake. The Old Wives' Tales also had gluten-free chocolate raspberry loaf, which was made of rice, fava, garbanzo and tapioca flours, brown sugar, coffee, eggs, soy oil, vanilla and chocolate chips. Then there was the gluten-free carrot cake loaf, made from rice, tapioca and potato flours, soy milk, eggs, carrots, pineapple, soy oil,

A photo of the very popular carrot cake. *Courtesy of photographer Scott Allen Tice.*

cloves, vanilla and baking soda. The number one favorite dessert of all time, according to Hart, was the Pumpkin Tofu Pudding, which was also vegan.

The Old Wives' Tales became known for catering to many people with food allergies at a time when many restaurants never considered the issue important. Personal remembrances include Rosalyn Newhouse recalling how important the dishes were as she and her daughter both had food allergies: "Back in the day, when my daughter was little and we were struggling with food allergies, the Old Wives' Tales was practically the only place in Portland we could be sure of getting a meal we could actually eat. The wait staff was so patient and helpful with us, figuring out what we could order. It was a real treat to be able to go out to eat and not worry about reactions. The children's play room was another great thing. Letting the kids enjoy themselves while the adults ordered and waited was a novel and welcome experience."

Another longtime customer, Sarah Gilbert, fondly remembered the kindness of Holly Hart when she was recovering from a pregnancy: "My brother's first wife (and my doula for my second child) was part of the tight circle Holly knew as family. I ended up having a partial placental abruption during my pregnancy, and Holly agreed to send me a twice-weekly abundance of food so I didn't have to cook while caring for my then-toddler and contending with my sensitive pregnancy. I still remember those cartons of mushroom soup and delicious goodies from the salad bar! Her generosity was amazing. The Old Wives' Tales holds such great memories of my little kids and other pregnant mamas."

Another mother, Katherine Sanderson Gray, remembered how nice it was to have the Old Wives' Tales nearby during the birth of her child: "Alma Birthing Center is just a few blocks away from where the Old Wives' Tales used to be. I had my second baby there, around 4:00 a.m., and a few hours later the midwives brought in a hearty and delicious breakfast for me. I don't remember much about the food—I think it was something like sausage and eggs—but I do remember being happy it was from Old Wives' Tales because I always felt like there was real *intention* in their food."

Much of Hart's passion for service work and social justice is reflected in what Julie L. Baumler, a longtime customer, remembered of her challenging youth and how Holly Hart positively impacted her life: "For many years, Holly let Windfire, the queer youth group, meet in her back room on Saturday afternoons. Windfire saved my sanity, and I have friends today that I met there."

But the Old Wives' Tales was also a safe haven for men, and that included fathers contending with their own challenges. Portland resident John Wilson remembered his visits: "Back in the day, I picked my kids up every other Thursday night for their five nights with Dad. It was great because the kids could run around that most wonderful play area and eat something healthy and tasty from the kids menu. As for me, after missing my kids and getting to see them, sitting there and being able to sip a cold beer made me feel human again after a heart-wrenching divorce."

The Old Wives' Tales was not without its share of drama though. Many past employees described Hart as a "tyrant" and abusive in much the same way Portland restaurant owners Henry Thiele or Horst Mager were described. Some former employees said that the Old Wives' Tales represented the most hostile working environment they had ever experienced, even going so far as to comment on a now defunct internet chat room to share war stories with other former employees. Many people seemed to either love or hate Hart, and there was rarely if ever an in-between.

As the years progressed and Hart grew older, the pace and demands of running a restaurant became too time-consuming and physically taxing. Hart closed the restaurant in 2014 and later sold the 1931 structure. It was demolished in 2015 and replaced with a sixty-nine-unit apartment building providing precious additional housing for Portland residents.

Many in Portland were genuinely saddened to learn that the Old Wives' Tales would be shuttering. They would be losing a favorite restaurant and hangout, which also meant losing access to their favorite vegetarian and vegan dishes. However, two of the recipes are shared at the end of this section for those who loved the food Holly Hart brought to her restaurant, including the beloved Hungarian Mushroom Soup, which was probably the best-known item on the Old Wives' Tales menu.

The Old Wives' Tales restaurant should always be remembered and honored for its owner and creator, Holly Hart, and for the dynamic role she played in strengthening Portland's gay community at a time when to be gay and open about it was discouraged. In a real and quantifiable way, Hart changed the landscape and the culture of Portland. The role she played in

Portland is remembered from an interview: "Holly should be considered the Founding Mother of Oregon's LGBTQ movement in general, and certainly one of the pioneer organizers in the women's community that developed."

Although the Old Wives' Tales is now gone, it will not be forgotten and will live on in the memories of its many fans. Despite having to be tough, as the owner and operator of such a busy and popular restaurant inevitably has to be, the legacy of Hart's social justice advocacy for the gay and lesbian community continues to affect the city that Portland has become. It is for these reasons that the important contributions Holly Hart made must never be forgotten.

This recipe for Hungarian Mushroom Soup comes from the *Moosewood Cookbook*.

Hungarian Mushroom Soup

Ingredients
2 cups onion, chopped
2 tablespoons vegetable stock
Salt
12 ounces of mushrooms, sliced
2 teaspoons dill weed
2 cups water
1 tablespoon tamari soy sauce
1 tablespoon Hungarian paprika
2 tablespoons butter
3 tablespoons flour
1 cup milk
Fresh ground black pepper to taste
1 half cup sour cream

Directions
Sauté onions in 2 tablespoons of stock and salt lightly. A few minutes later, add mushrooms, 1 teaspoon dill, ½ cup water, soy sauce and paprika. Cover and simmer 15 minutes. Melt butter in large saucepan. Whisk in flour and cook, whisking a few minutes. Add milk and cook, stirring frequently, over low heat about 10 minutes, until thick. Stir in mushroom mixture and remaining stock. Cover and simmer 10–15 minutes. Just before serving, add salt, pepper, sour cream and, if desired, extra dill (1 teaspoon). Serve garnished with parsley.

• • • •

A favorite dessert recipe was provided by Holly Hart, included here.

Swedish Cream with Fresh Berries

INGREDIENTS
3 cups sour cream
½ cup white sugar
½ cup plain yogurt (better if not Greek yogurt)
1 teaspoon vanilla
2 cups heavy cream

DIRECTIONS
Mix well in a bowl: sour cream, sugar, yogurt and vanilla. Heat cream in a saucepan to just below boiling (scald). Slowly add heated cream to other ingredients, whipping until thoroughly combined. Chill in the refrigerator before serving over the fresh berries of your choice. This can also be used as a sauce over various cakes.

• • • •

CAFÉ LENA, 1991–2001

Café Lena burst onto the restaurant and literary scene on April 3, 1991, with a resounding and appreciative welcome from residents all across Portland. The famously eclectic restaurant became something of a legend as a popular place to hang out and enjoy excellent food and intellectually stimulating company. In no time at all, Café Lena became known nationwide as a place where people could get big sandwiches, big salads, fine wine, excellent baked desserts and pastries and also listen to some of the most inventive modern free verse that Portland and the Pacific Northwest had to offer. Café Lena, located at 2239 Southeast Hawthorne Boulevard, was the brainchild of married couple Steve Sander and Leanne Grabel and remained in operation for a bit over ten years, celebrating the spoken word and great food.

Left: A colorful Café Lena menu. *Courtesy of Steve Sander and Leanne Grabel.*

Below: A busy day outside Café Lena. *Courtesy of Steve Sander and Leanne Grabel.*

The name Café Lena was created by combining the first names of both of the owners' young children, Lili and Gina, in honor of their two pretty daughters. People sometimes wonder if Café Lena became a restaurant first and a hangout for aspiring and established poets later, but the reality is that it was created with the idea in mind to always be a place where poets could socialize and support one another and eat nutritious food. Grabel and Sander had wanted to create a place where people could gather and nourish themselves on quality wholesome food, as well as share their poetry with an eager audience.

With Café Lena's location in the heart of the Hawthorne district, it was one of the most happening places in Portland and became the hub of the nearby residential neighborhood, with people flooding in for breakfast and lunch, particularly on the weekend morning rushes. Leanne Grabel (a writer, illustrator, performance poet and semi-retired special education teacher) and her husband, Steve Sander (a musician, songwriter, poet and editor of the literary review *Spectrum Magazine*) shared their thoughts on why they opened Café Lena in a 2019 interview.

Grabel explained how they opened up the café at a time when rent for commercial space was not exorbitant and when such a business venture not as risky as it would be today: "We were at the Mount Hood Jazz Festival in 1990, and we ran into a friend and he said that he owned this building on Twenty-Third and Hawthorne. There was a pizza parlor there, and it was the first whole wheat crust in Portland, Porretta's Pizza, owned by Gary Slac. Gary wanted to sell and move out, and it was like this spontaneous idea of 'Maybe we should open a poetry place!'—even though neither of us had ever done anything with restaurants at all. But we were involved with the poetry scene and the theater scene. And it was cheap; it was like $300 or $400 a month. It seemed doable."

Neither Leanne nor Steve had any previous experience operating a restaurant, but they did have intelligence, a genuine collaborative interest and great friends to help guide them along the way with ideas, recipes and support. This included Mike Weinstein, who created all the breads and pasta recipes, including the first eastside challah, which quickly became a popular Café Lena favorite.

Leanne and Steve began to get the help they needed from friends who shared recipes and volunteered to work as cooks, all while creating space for poets and musicians. "The idea was to do a poetry place," Grabel remembered. "The restaurant aspect was secondary, but the café turned out to be a restaurant with three meals a day, an in-house baker and so on. I'm sure the open mic started within two weeks of opening. It lasted the whole ten years. The first night it was packed!"

Celebrated Portland writer Monica Drake, writing for the *Portland Mercury* in 2001, recalled in an elegantly written review some of the delectable dishes from the dinner menu that were offered at Café Lena:

> *The salmon special was served with capers and a light sauce that was fresh yet rich. It came with a generous helping of delicate basil rice, and garnished with lightly steamed asparagus. Chicken for Charles Bukowski is recommendable, with red peppers, tender chicken, and cream sauce. The tossed salad is made of the same lovely curls of mesculin we've come to expect from Lena, enhanced with the surprise of toasted, sugared walnuts. The second salad option is heartier, with wild rice, chopped vegetables and sweet currents. The desserts are wonderful and basic. Chocolate cake, cheese cake, coconut cream pie.*

Other dishes included simple breakfast with amusing names like Still No Money, which was a simple plate for $4.50: "Two eggs as you like them, pile of spuds & delicious Lena toast or scone." Then there was Steve's

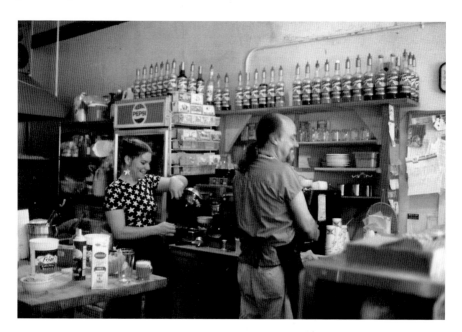

Steve Sander hard at work. *Courtesy of Steve Sander and Leanne Grabel.*

Egg Breakfast for $5.50: "Two eggs scrambled w/scallions, mushrooms & cheddar w/spuds & delicious Lena toast or scone."

Sandwiches—which also had amusing names—were large and filled with generous amounts of cheese, meat and vegetables. There was the Venetian ("garlicky, basil-touched sicillian-marinated eggplant, provolone, parmesan baked on baguette"), the Basque ("creamy Dijon, fresh tomatoes, & brie baked on crusty baguette), the Sweet Basque ("...with pears instead of tomatoes"), the Sicilian ("Sicilian meatballs, sweet red sauce, mozzarella & parmesan baked on baguette") and the Birkenstock ("pesto mayo, a myriad of grilled vegetables & provolone & cheddar baked on baguette"). There were also several other sandwiches, including the Pizzarina ("grilled garlic, sweet Sicillian red sauce, mozzarella & parmesan & a sprinkle of parsley").

Writer Steffen Silvis recalled Café Lena in an excellent 2001 *Willamette Week* review: "Considering we live in a country whose historical memory rarely exceeds last week, there are a surprising number of restaurants in Portland that have defied the fashion of disposability. Café Lena, the matrix of Portland's spoken-word movement, has recently passed into its third ownership, but outwardly remains Lena in look (if not appeal)."

Silvis further elaborated on the allure of Café Lena and its popularity even after it had changed owners:

> *Café Lena has long been a fixture of Southeast Hawthorne Boulevard. This Mecca for Moderns and Beats slung cheap, delectable hash while offering a platform for hopeful wordsmiths to air their wares. The new owner, Karen Harding, has kept the dish names (christened after writers) as well as much of Lena's bric-a-brac. Tables are still inlaid with writers' mug shots and scraps of poems. And the front door is still one of the most eclectic portrait galleries in town. Harding, who owns the popular Cup and Saucer on Hawthorne and the Dahlia Café on Northeast Killingsworth Street, has made some needed changes to the cafe's layout, adding more room for both customers and kitchen staff. She's also brightened the room by slapping a coat of mustard brown over the aubergine purple that used to cover the wainscot.*

Open mic nights at Café Lena could get busy. The energy was often chaotic and exciting as people approached the mic and began reciting their poetical creations. Sometimes there was music, and a poetry slam atmosphere reigned as people rapped out their poems. There were many

The beautiful interior of Café Lena. *Courtesy of Steve Sander and Leanne Grabel.*

well-known poets who regularly read at Café Lena and are still residing in Portland today, writing and publishing, including Judith Barrington, Casey Bush, Tim Barnes, Barbara LaMorticella, Doug Spangle, Walt Curtis and, of course, the phenomenal and prolific poet Mr. Dan Raphael!

Steve Sander remembered the fun of running Café Lena:

> *I remember the first week we were both standing behind the counter, and Leanne was standing right next to me and she goes: "What have we done? I can't even stand people!" And I was like, "Listen to this room, it's just buzzing!" It was very good for us, branching out and doing something else. You know, I felt like I raised another ten or twelve kids at the end of it all. We had some of the folks there with us the whole ten years. They started when they were nineteen and then they were twenty-nine! It was a good bunch. We had a really cool group. But Café Lena was like the universe coming into place. We felt we were meant to do this—it was meant to happen! Tuesday nights and the weekends were our busiest nights. Brian Booth came by; Ani DiFranco came by before she was known. Culturally, it was a really cool scene at Café Lena.*

172

The daughter of Leanne Grabel and Steve Sander, Gina Sander, provided nostalgic and charming detail of what Café Lena meant to her in a long remembrance that covers much of the magic of the busy and popular restaurant:

I was 11 months old when the café opened, and it closed after my 11th birthday. It was a short walk from my elementary school. This meant I could easily pop down after school and get a strawberry Italian soda—no cream! I liked watching the grownups work and seeing my dad work the grill. I don't think I'll ever eat a turkey sandwich as good as the ones I had at Café Lena. My memories are about the small details, maybe because I was a small person for the duration of the cafe's existence. I remember the shelf of Italian soda syrup and the thrill when I was old enough to read the titles of each flavor. The bright pink and blue neon sign that hung in the window and the spooky papier-mâché puppet that sat above one of the windows. My usual order was a turkey and provolone or Swiss on challah with mayo and sprouts—still one of my favorite sandwich ingredients to date. On poetry open mic nights I'd usually bring a friend, Hanna Hallman. Hanna and I felt like queens in our own play-palace. We'd wander through the kitchen, running our imaginary restaurant, or stand at the cash register and mimic the movements we'd see adults do. "That'll be five dollars! (beep boop!) Here is your change and have a good day!" One of my all-time favorite errands with my dad was shopping for the cafe. We'd hit Sheridan Fruit, where I was allowed to buy a small bag of white cheddar popcorn—I'm sure a small distraction to keep me entertained while we roamed through the store grabbing flats of fruits and veggies. Then we'd stop at Cash & Carry, now called Smart Foods, and I'd sit at the back of the flat cart shifting where I sat as we added boxes, jugs, bags of chips, straws and to-go containers. Once we made it to the dairy cooler, my dad would hand me a mini chocolate milk—my second prize of the day for "helping." I have always been so proud to be part of that place and of my incredible parents, who fed this city challah French toast before it was cool.

Remembering those busy years, Grabel also recalled the role Café Lena played in nurturing the poetry communities in Portland. "Poetry wise, I think Café Lena had a vital role in Portland's poetry scene. A lot of people got their start, a lot of people got their husbands and wives involved, and it just generated a lot of stuff."

The Café Lena gang on a sunny day. *Courtesy of Steve Sander and Leanne Grabel.*

After Café Lena had been in business for a number of years, it changed hands and was bought and sold by friends. Eventually, the café closed after ten full years, and this once bright mecca for delicious food and some of the best poetry in town was shuttered. An entire community mourned the closing of Café Lena, knowing that they had lived through a special and explosively creative time in Portland history that they would never be able to replicate in quite the same way again.

Bibliography

Sourcing for this book came primarily through the *Oregonian* historical archive at the Multnomah County Library, *Willamette Week* online and personal interviews conducted with former restaurant owners, managers, employees and customers.

Introduction

Abbott, Carl. *Portland in Three Centuries: The Place and the People*. Corvallis: Oregon State University Press, 2011. http://osupress.oregonstate.edu/sites/default/files/Abbott.PortlandinThreeCenturies.excerpt.pdf.

Applegate, Jesse. "Recollections of My Boyhood." Internet Archives. https://archive.org/stream/GR_75/GR_75_djvu.txt.

ISSUU. "A People's History of Portland: Know Your City Shares the Stories of Portland Immigrant, Working Class and Activist Roots." https://issuu.com/travelportland/docs/know_your_city_a_people_s_history_o.

Louie, James. Interview with Theresa Griffin Kennedy, Oregon, February 2019.

Portland, Oregon. Archives and Records Management, 1843–1901. https://www.portlandoregon.gov/archives/article/284518.

Willingham, William F. "U.S. Army Corps of Engineers." *Oregon Encyclopedia*, last updated January 22, 2021. https://oregonencyclopedia.org/articles/u_s__army_corps_of_engineers/#.XF3cw1xKjIU.

Wulff, Alexia. "Portland Oregon's Various Nicknames and Where They Came From." Culture Trip, January 29, 2017. https://theculturetrip.com/north-america/usa/oregon/articles/portland-oregons-various-nicknames-and-where-they-came-from.

The Vegetarian Restaurant

Anderson, A. Heather. *Portland: A Food Biography*. Lanham, MD: Rowman & Littlefield, 2014.

Aoyagi, A., and W. Shurtleff. "History of Seventh Day Adventist Work with Soyfoods, Vegetarianism, Meat Alternatives, Wheat Gluten, Dietary Fiber and Peanut Butter (1893–2013)." Extensively annotated bibliography and sourcebook. Soy Info Center, 2014. https://www.soyinfocenter.com/pdf/172/Adve.pdf.

Brooks, Karen, Tuck Woodstock, and Michael Zusman. "Pioneer Salt, Giant Pancakes, and Sexy Salads: The Two-Century-Long Story of How Portland Conquered the Food World." *Portland Monthly*, September 2016. https://www.pdxmonthly.com/articles/2016/8/15/pioneer-salt-giant-pancakes-and-sexy-salads-the-two-century-long-story-of-how-portland-conquered-the-food-world.

La Ganga, Maria. "The World's First Vegan Mini-Mall. Yeah, You're in Portland." *Los Angeles Times*, May 4, 2015. https://www.latimes.com/nation/la-na-vegan-mini-mall-20150504-story.html.

Oregonian. "ADVENTIST CAMPMEETING: A Vegetarian Restaurant Doing a Good Business." May 23, 1898.

———. "Prospects Were Slim: Little Encouragement for Promoter of Vegetarian Restaurant." January 17, 1898.

———. "Vegetarian Restaurant; Portland Eating House Which Sells No Meat." March 28, 1900.

Shurtleff, William, and Akiko Aoyagi. "Small Adventist Food Companies and Sanitariums: Work with Soybeans." Soy Info Center, 2004. http://www.soyinfocenter.com/HSS/small_adventist_food_companies.php.

Washington Adventist Hospital. "Mind, Body, Spirit, Health: Celebrating 100 Years." 2007. https://www.adventisthealthcare.com/app/files/public/ea5ad9ec-7694-4503-84ef-52eecfce9c0a/pdf-WAH-100-Years-Book.pdf.

Manning's Coffee Café

Cram, Justin. "The Relighting of Manning's Coffee Shop Sign." KCET, January 11, 2012. https://www.kcet.org/history-society/the-relighting-of-mannings-coffee-shop-sign.

Geni. "Edward McClure Manning, Sr." November 8, 2018. https://www.geni.com/people/Edward-Manning-Sr/6000000083793180141.

Hunt, Brian J. Interview with Theresa Griffin Kennedy, Oregon, 2019.

Manning's Kitchen. "History." http://www.manningskitchen.com/history.

Mershon, Andrew. "Restless Easterner Began Manning Restaurant Chain." *Oregonian*, April 9, 1972.

Mohai Museum of History and Industry. "Manning's Coffee Shop on Market Street, Seattle, Circa 1947." https://digitalcollections.lib.washington.edu/digital/collection/imlsmohai/id/11025.

Morris, Nancy. "Hints on Coffee Making Told by Andrew C. Glover." *Oregonian*, August 25, 1959.

Noles, BJ. "Lloyd Center Deer Draws Crowd." *Oregonian*, June 17, 1978.

Oregonian. "Manning Brothers Started Huge Chain in Small Seattle Shop." July 26, 1964.

Pemberton, Tracy. "Manning's Success Formula." Unpublished manuscript, California, 2017.

Sunday Oregonian. "Thieves Enter Café." April 14, 1957.

The Lotus Cardroom and Café

Alborn, Denise M. "Crimping and Shanghaiing on the Columbia River." *Oregon Historical Quarterly* 93, no. 3 (1992): 262–91. http://www.jstor.org/stable/20614468.

Andrews, Reed. "After 92 Years Downtown's Portland's Lotus Bar to Close for High-Rise Hotel Project." KATU 2, August 2, 2016. https://katu.com/news/local/after-92-years-sw-portlands-lotus-bar-to-close-for-high-rise-hotel-project.

Bamman, Mattie John. "The Lotus Cardroom and Café to Shutter after 92 Years." Eater Portland, Oregon, August 2016. https://pdx.eater.com/2016/8/3/12368308/lotus-cardroom-and-cafe-to-shutter-closing.

Bancud, Michaela. "Lotus Card Room Building May Fold for Good." Business Tribune Pamplin Media Group, December 1, 2015. https://pamplinmedia.com/but/239-news/283389-159086-lotus-card-room-building-may-fold-for-good.

"Brunswick-Balke-Collender Company." *Encyclopedia Dubuque*, December 7, 2019. http://www.encyclopediadubuque.org/index. php?title=BRUNSWICK-BALKE-COLLENDER_COMPANY.

Butler, Grant. "Demolition Begins on Downtown's Historic Lotus Building." *Oregonian*, June 28, 2018. https://www.oregonlive.com/expo/news/erry-2018/06/053ea8a1ae4099/demolition_begins_on_downtowns.html.

Chronicle. "Offbeat Oregon: Portland's 'Shanghai Tunnels' Are Mostly Myth, but Not Entirely." May 29, 2019. https://www.chronicle1909. com/posts/2024/offbeat-oregon-portlands-shanghai-tunnels-are-mostly-myth-but-not-entirely.

Dillon, H. Richard. *Shanghaiing Days*. N.p.: Silverstowe, 2012.

DuPay, Don. Interview with Theresa Griffin Kennedy, Oregon, 2019.

Engeman, Richard. "Shanghaiing in Portland and the Shanghai Tunnel Myth." *Oregon Encyclopedia*. https://oregonencyclopedia.org/articles/shanghai_tunnels_myth/#.XGonc-hKjIV.

Finn, J.D. John. "P-Town's Shanghai Tunnels Mostly Myth…or Are They?" *Offbeat Oregon History*, May 26, 2019. http://offbeatoregon. com/1905d.shanghai-tunnels-based-on-true-story-549.html.

Frane, Alex. "See the Lotus Cardroom's 130-Year-Old Bar in New Home in McMenamins." Eater Portland, Oregon, October 13, 2017. https://pdx.eater.com/2017/10/13/16462238/lotus-cardroom-bar-mcmenamins-photos-pdx.

Jung, Helen. "Portland's Buried Truth. Historians Say the Story of the City's Infamous Shanghai Tunnels Likely Is a Myth." *Oregonian*, October 4, 2007. https://web.archive.org/web/20071012113433/http://www.oregonlive.com/news/oregonian/index.ssf?%2Fbase%2Fnews%2F1191466510318550.xml&coll=7.

Karns, Anna. Interview with Theresa Griffin Kennedy, Oregon, 2014.

King, Shelby R. "Say Goodbye to Two Pieces of Portland History." *Portland Mercury*, December 2, 2015. https://www.portlandmercury. com/portland/say-goodbye-to-two-pieces-of-portland-history/Content?oid=17084635.

Oregonian. "Ascher Beats Lawrence. Portlander Wins Opening Games of Billiard Tournament." November 11, 1910.

———. "Bartender, 58, Shot to Death." October 30, 1979.

———. "CLOTHIERS GET NEW SITE: Buffum & Pendleton to Occupy Old Home of Lotus Café." August 9, 1916.

———. "SALOON UNDER FIRE. Prosecutor Has Four Fined and Says He Is After Others." July 25, 1914.

———. "Trial Begins in Lotus Killing." February 22, 1979.

Peterson Loomis, Jacqueline. "Oregon's Infamous Shanghai Tunnels Likely Mythical." *Ashland Tidings*, 2007. https://www.ashlandtidings.com/lifestyle/2007/10/10/oregons-infamous-shanghai-tunnels-likely-mythical.

Pintarich, Paul. *History by the Glass*. N.p.: Bianco Publishing, 1986.

Vincent, John. "Historic Struggle." *Business Tribune*, January 29, 2016. https://pamplinmedia.com/but/239-news/291810-167683-historic-struggle.

Wilson, Steven. "Of Crimes and Shanghaied Sailors." HistoryNet. https://www.historynet.com/of-crimes-and-shanghaied-sailors.htm.

Yaw's Top Notch

Ashton, David F. "New 'Yaw's Top Notch' Packed with Diners—Before 'Grand Opening.'" *East Portland News*, 2012. https://eastpdxnews.com/general-news-features/new-yaws-top-notch-packed-with-diners-before-grand-opening.

DuPay, Don. Interview with Theresa Griffin Kennedy, Oregon, February 7, 2019.

Fehrenbacher, Lee. "Yaw's Top Notch Burger Joint to Reopen in Northeast Portland." DJC Oregon, May 11, 2012. http://djcoregon.com/news/2012/05/11/yaws-top-notch-burger-joint-to-reopen-in-northeast-portland.

Portland History. "The House that Hamburger Built." March 12, 2013. http://www.pdxhistory.com/html/yaw_s_top_notch.html.

Russell, Michael. "Steven P. Yaw, Grandson of Yaw's Top Notch Founder, Dies at 70." Oregon Live, March 16, 2017. https://www.oregonlive.com/dining/index.ssf/2017/03/steven_p_yaw_grandson_of_yaws.html.

Stumptown Blogger. "Early Yaw's Top Notch Menu." July 16, 2010. https://www.stumptownblogger.com/2010/07/early-yaws-top-notch-menu.html.

Swart, Cornelius. "In East Portland, Yaw's Top Notch Drive-in Stakes a Comeback on Nostalgia for When the Car Was King." Oregon Live, August 23, 2012. https://www.oregonlive.com/portland/2012/08/in_east_portland_yaws_top_notc.html.

The Monte Carlo

Chilson, John. "Lost: The Monte Carlo on Belmont." Lost Oregon, 2008. https://lostoregon.org/2008/10/24/the-monte-carlo-on-belmont.

Hungry Browser. "Uncle Phaedrus: Consulting Detective and Finder of Lost Recipes." 2014. http://www.hungrybrowser.com/phaedrus/m1128F14.htm.

Stewart, Fred. Interview with Theresa Griffin Kennedy, Oregon, March 10, 2019.

Wegner, Chris. Interview with Theresa Griffin Kennedy, Oregon, May 8, 2019.

Henry Thiele's Restaurant

Armstrong, J.A. *Dining à la Oregon: A Guide to Eating Adventures in Oregon Restaurants, Featuring Famous Recipes for Specialties of the House.* N.p.: J&K Publishing Company, 1959.

Beard, James. *Delights and Prejudices.* Philadelphia: Running Press, 2001.

Clark, Rachel. Interview with Theresa Griffin Kennedy, Oregon, 2019.

Engeman, Richard. "Henry Thiele 1882–1952." *Oregon Encyclopedia*, last updated 2021. https://oregonencyclopedia.org/articles/thiele-henry/#.XM_LQY5KjIU.

———. "The Land of Princess Charlotte." *Oregon Rediviva*, April 4, 2015. http://oregonrediviva.blogspot.com/2015/04/the-land-of-princess-charlotte.html.

Fisher, Gerald. *The Scalawag: The Long Life and Times of Gerald John Fisher.* N.p.: CreateSpace Independent Publishing Platform, 2015.

Taber, C. Perri. Interview with Theresa Griffin Kennedy, Oregon, 2019.

The Georgian Room

Butler, Grant. "Tasty Memories: 97 Long-Gone Portland Restaurants We Wish Were Still Around." *Oregonian,* archived from the original on December 28, 2020.

Curran, Christine. "Oregon Places: The Georgian Room at Meier & Frank." *Oregon Historical Quarterly* 107, no. 3 (Fall 2006): 438–44.

Falcioni, Pamela. Interview with Theresa Griffin Kennedy, Oregon, October 2019.

Moore, Mark. "Meet Me Under the Clock." Portland History, 2013. http://www.pdxhistory.com/html/meier___frank.html.

Fryer's Quality Pie

Adams, Shauna. Interview with Theresa Griffin Kennedy, May 15, 2019.

Chilson, John. "Portland's Restaurant Heritage." Lost Oregon, 2010. https://lostoregon.org/2010/05/30/portlands-restaurant-heritage.

Flowers, Lisa. Interview with Theresa Griffin Kennedy, 2021.

Gunderson, Laurel. Interview with Theresa Griffin Kennedy, May 15, 2019.

Kennedy, John. Interview with Theresa Griffin Kennedy, May 14, 2019.

Kofler, Roger. Interview with Theresa Griffin Kennedy, May 14, 2019.

Korn, Peter. "Northwest Portland Sites Sits Barren Amidst Bustle." *Business Tribune*, 2007. https://pamplinmedia.com/component/content/article?id=95394.

Miller, Alexis Sara. Interview with Theresa Griffin Kennedy, May 15, 2019.

The Chocolate Lounge/Orange Slice

Department Store Museum. "Lipman's." 2012. http://www.thedepartment storemuseum.org/2010/06/limpmans-portland-oregon.html.

5th Avenue Suites Hotel. "Our Downtown Portland, Oregon Hotel Is an Architectural Gem." https://web.archive.org/web/20050928115015/http://www.5thavenuesuites.com/fashist.

Moore, Mark. "Lipman Wolf & Company." Portland History. http://www.pdxhistory.com/html/lipman_wolfe.html.

Oregonian. "Frederick & Nelson Stores Taken Over." August 28, 1987.

———. "Tonight We Close Our Doors as Lipman's…" Advertisement, March 30, 1979, A3.

Portland History. "Department Story." http://www.pdxhistory.com/html/department_stores.html.

———. "Frederick Nelson." http://www.pdxhistory.com/html/frederick_-_nelson.html.

Waddle's Coffee Shop

KATU 2. "Waddle's Shuts Down After Nearly 60 Years in Business." 2006. https://katu.com/news/local/waddles-shuts-down-after-nearly-60-years-in-business.

Libby, Brian. "What Price Donuts?" *Willamette Week*, April 2003. https://www.wweek.com/portland/article-1979-what-price-donuts.html.

Loomans, Taz. "The Understated and Awe Inspiring Churches of Pietro Belluschi." Blooming Rock, 2013. http://bloomingrock.com/2013/11/19/the-understated-and-awe-inspiring-churches-of-pietro-belluschi.

Portland History. "Waddle's." http://www.pdxhistory.com/html/waddles.html.

Uniquely Portland Oregon. "Waddle's Restaurant in Portland Oregon." http://www.uniquely-portland-oregon.com/waddles-restaurant.html.

DuPay's Drive-In Restaurant

DuPay, Don. Interview with Theresa Griffin Kennedy, Oregon, 2019.

The Hollywood Burger Bar

DeRouchie, Jonie. Interview with Theresa Griffin Kennedy, 2019.

Elliot, Craig. Interview with Theresa Griffin Kennedy, Oregon, 2019.

Kleinman, Geoff. "The Original Burger at Hollywood Burger Bar." *On Portland, Entertainment, Arts, Culture and Food*, 2010. https://www.onpdx.com/food/the-original-burger-at-hollywood-burger-bar-reviewing-the-dish.

Korfhage, Matthew. "Snoop Dogg's Uncle Reo Bought the 60-Year-Old Hollywood Burger Bar Goodbye Burgers. Hello Reo's Ribs." *Willamette Week*, 2015. https://www.wweek.com/restaurants/2015/10/05/snoop-doggs-uncle-reo-bought-the-60-year-old-hollywood-burger-bar.

Neeson, Fred. Interview with Theresa Griffin Kennedy, Oregon, 2019.

Russell, Michael. "Hollywood Burger Bar Closes After 61 Years in NE Portland; Reo's Ribs Moves In." *Oregonian*, 2015. https://www.oregonlive.com/dining/2015/10/ne_portlands_hollywood_burger.html.

Sambo's Restaurant

Atomic Redhead—Unusual Destinations, Weird History and More. "History of Sambo's Restaurant." 2018. https://atomicredhead.com/2018/02/26/history-of-sambos-restaurant.

Budds, Diana. "The Ultimate Guide to Googie; How LA Got Its Grooviest Architecture." *Curbed*, July 24, 2019. https://www.curbed.com/2019/7/24/18647602/the-ultimate-guide-to-googie#intro.

Champion, Edward. "Racist Restaurants." Reluctant Habits, 2007. http://www.edrants.com/racist-restaurants.

Golus, Carrie. "Sambo's Subtext: An Unsettling but Enduring Children's Book Is the Subject of a New Special Collections Exhibit." *University of Chicago Magazine* (2010). http://magazine.uchicago.edu/1010/chicago_journal/sambos-subtext.shtml.

Heritage Auctions. "Helen Bannerman—The Story of Little Black Sambo." https://historical.ha.com/itm/books/children-s-books/helen-bannerman-the-story-of-little-black-sambo-london-grant-richards-1899-first-edition-ownership/a/6234-45170.s.

LaMotte, Greg. "Sambo's Revival Running into Hot Water." CNN, 1998. http://edition.cnn.com/US/9801/28/sambo.revival/#1.

Loganberry Books. "Helen Bannerman." http://www.loganberrybooks.com/books/authors/helen-bannerman.htm.

Metz, Robert. "Market Place; Mistakes at Sambo's." *New York Times*, November 27, 1981. https://www.nytimes.com/1981/11/27/business/market-place-mistakes-at-sambo-s.html.

Novak, Matt. "Googie: Architecture of the Space Age." *Smithsonian Magazine* (2012). https://www.smithsonianmag.com/history/googie-architecture-of-the-space-age-122837470.

Palminteri, John. "It's Official—Chad's Replaces Sambo's After 63 Years in Santa Barbara." News Channel 3, 2020. https://keyt.com/news/money-and-business/2020/07/15/its-official-chads-replaces-sambos-after-63-years-in-santa-barbara/#:~:text=SANTA%20BARBARA%2C%20Calif.,Sambo's%20restaurant%20is%20now%20Chad's.

Pollard, Jessica. "Restaurant in Lincoln City Under Fire for Its Name." *Street Roots*, 2020. https://www.streetroots.org/news/2020/07/05/restaurant-lincoln-city-under-fire-its-name.

Romano, Andrew. "Pancakes and Pickaninnies: The Saga of 'Sambo's,' the 'Racist' Restaurant Chain America Once Loved." *Daily Beast*, 2017. https://www.thedailybeast.com/pancakes-and-pickaninnies-the-saga-of-sambos-the-racist-restaurant-chain-america-once-loved.

Sambo's Family Restaurant. "Architectural Design." http://www. sambosonline.com/sambos_googie.htm.

Sircar, Sanjay "Little Brown Sanjay and Little Black Sambo." *Lion and the Unicorn* 28, no. 1 (January 2004). Baruch College, CUNY. https://blogs. baruch.cuny.edu/inshort/files/2015/03/small_Little_Brown_Sanjay_ and_Little_Black_Sambo.pdf.

Stumptown Blogger. "Sambo's on 23rd and Burnside." 2012. https://www. stumptownblogger.com/2012/03/sambos-on-23rd-burnside.html.

Whitaker, Jan. "Name Trouble—Sambos.'" *Restaurant-ing Through History*, 2013. https://restaurant-ingthroughhistory.com/2013/09/02/name-trouble-sambos.

Zhang, Jenny G. "California Breakfast Spot Sambo's Will Change Its Name Following Community Demands." Eater Portland, Oregon, 2020. https://www.eater.com/2020/6/9/21285192/santa-barbara-breakfast-chain-sambos-name-change-black-lives-matter.

Club 21

Bakall, Samantha. "Beloved Dive Bar Club 21 Closing This Weekend." *Oregonian*, January 2017. https://www.oregonlive.com/dining/index. ssf/2017/01/beloved_dive_bar_club_21_closi.html.

Bamman, Mattie John. "Portland Dive Bar that Looks Like Snow White's House Officially Doomed." Eater Portland, Oregon, 2017. https:// pdx.eater.com/2017/1/9/14220048/club-21-officially-closing-dive-bar-portland.

Cole, David B. "Russian Oregon: A History of the Russian Orthodox Church and Settlement in Oregon, 1882–1976." Thesis, Portland State University, 1976. Paper 2334, via PDXScholar. https://doi. org/10.15760/etd.2331.

Find A Grave. "Jacob Lewis 'Jake' Freiman." https://www.findagrave. com/memorial/106938581/jacob-lewis-freiman.

———. "Paul George Bulkin." https://www.findagrave.com/ memorial/66309852/paul-george-bulkin.

Korfhage, Matthew. "Club 21 Will Be Demolished to Become Apartments, After Owners Sign Over Remaining Decade of Lease." *Willamette Week*, January 9, 2017. https://www.wweek.com/bars/news-bars/2017/01/09/club-21-will-be-demolished-to-become-apartments-after-owners-sign-over-remaining-decade-of-lease.

Lannamann, Ned. "Portland Dive Bar Club 21 Might Be Moving—
    Building and All." *Portland Mercury*, October 14, 2016. https://www.
    portlandmercury.com/blogtown/2016/10/14/18631700/portland-
    dive-bar-club-21-might-be-movingbuilding-and-all.
———. "Yes, It's True: Iconic Portland Dive Bar Club 21 Is Closing."
    Portland Mercury, January 9, 2017. https://www.portlandmercury.com/
    blogtown/2017/01/09/18780970/yes-its-true-iconic-portland-dive-bar-
    club-21-is-closing.
Reimers and Jolivette. "Historical Renovations." 2020. http://www.
    reimersandjolivette.com.

The Burger Barn

Dawdy, Philip, and Grant Menzies. "1981." *Willamette Week*, 2005. https://
    www.wweek.com/portland/article-4180-1981.html.
Law, Steve. "Walking with Civil Rights Pioneers." *Business Tribune*, 2013.
    https://pamplinmedia.com/pt/9-news/129905-walking-with-civil-
    rights-pioneers?tmpl=component.
March, Tanya Lyn. "Mrs. Katherine Gray Founder of the Harriet Tubman
    Club: Lived in the Burger Barn Building." Historic Preservation Club,
    June 26, 2014. http://historicpreservationclub.blogspot.com/2014/06/
    mrs-katherine-gray-founder-of-harriet.html.
MLK in Motion. "Black and Blue in Albina, Part 2: The Burger
    Barn Opossums on Union Avenue." November 12, 2015. https://
    mlkinmotion.wordpress.com/2015/11/12/black-and-blue-in-albina-pt-
    2-the-burger-barn-opossums-on-union-avenue.
———. "Christopher's Gourmet Grill." May 26, 2013. https://
    mlkinmotion.wordpress.com/2013/05/26/christophers-gourmet-grill-3.
Mungen. "Burger Barn Possum Incident." YouTube, May 25, 2017.
    https://www.youtube.com/watch?v=54v5GW5h_rk.
Oregonian. "Colored Suffragists Act." September 17, 1912, 12. Via
    Century of Action, Deschutes County Historical Society. http://
    centuryofaction.org/index.php/main_site/News_Articles/colored_
    suffragists_act.
Silvis, Helen. "Century of Action Shines Light on Black Suffragist Hattie
    Redmond." *Skanner*, May 10, 2012. https://www.theskanner.com/news/
    northwest/14242-century-of-action-shines-light-on-black-suffragist-
    hattie-redmond-2012-05-10.

UPI. "The Black Owners of a NE Portland Restaurant Have…." December 5, 1981. https://www.upi.com/Archives/1981/12/05/The-black-owners-of-a-northeast-Portland-restaurant-have/5891376376400.

The Barbary Coast/Hoyt Hotel

Chilson, John. "The Barbary Coast at the Hoyt Hotel." Lost Oregon, 2008. https://lostoregon.org/2008/09/09/the-barbary-coast-at-the-hoyt-hotel.
Haneckow, Dan. "Pettycoat Junction Mysteries." Train Orders, 2011. https://www.trainorders.com/discussion/read.php?11,2609522.
———. "Portland Xanadu: The Rise and Fall of the Hoyt Hotel." *Oregon Encyclopedia*, 2013. http://blog.oregonlive.com/my-portland/2013/05/portland_xanadu_the_rise_and_f.html.
Horn, Don. "Gracie Diana Hansen, 1922–1985." *Oregon Encyclopedia*, 2021. https://oregonencyclopedia.org/articles/hansen_gracie/#.XjDP02hKjIU.
Laquedem, Isaac. "Harvey Dick." *Keep Oregon Blue*, 2004. https://isaac.blogs.com/isaac_laquedem/2004/12/harvey_dick.html.
Marshal, Cathy. "Gracie Hansen Honors Portland Legend." KGW, 2012.
Puget Sound Pipeline. "Barbary Coast Restaurant Fotoplayer." 2004. http://www.pstos.org/instruments/or/portland/barbary-coast.htm.
Stumptown Blogger. "Harvey Dicks Hoyt Hotel & Barbary Coast Gay Nineties Showroom." 2012. https://www.stumptownblogger.com/2012/02/harvey-dicks-hoyt-hotel-barbary-coast-gay-nineties-showroom.html.
———. "The Roaring 20s Room at the Hoyt Hotel." 2010. https://www.stumptownblogger.com/2010/04/the-roaring-20s-room-at-the-hoyt-hotel.html.
Wikipedia. "Hoyt Hotel." https://en.wikipedia.org/wiki/Hoyt_Hotel.

The River Queen

Alderson, George. Interview with Theresa Griffin Kennedy, 2019.
Baldwin, Debra Hagen. Interview with Theresa Griffin Kennedy, 2019.
Beardsley, Michael. "The River Queen…What Happened to the Grand Lady?" Stumptown Blogger, 2009. https://www.stumptownblogger.com/2009/11/the-river-queenwhat-happened-to-the-grand-lady.html.

Chalmers, Keely. "Coast Guard Cleaning Up 'River Queen,' Other Derelict Boats on Columbia." KGW Channel 8, 2017. https://www.kgw.com/article/news/local/coast-guard-cleaning-up-river-queen-other-derelict-boats-on-columbia/283-446104810.

Crowell, Doug. Interview with Theresa Griffin Kennedy, 2019.

Howard, John William. "Ghost Queen: Story of the Forgotten River Queen." *Business Tribune*, 2015. https://pamplinmedia.com/pt/11-features/269917-144702-ghost-queen-story-of-the-forgotten-river-queen.

Kamiya, Gary. "When the Flow of Traffic Was All Aboard the Ferries." *San Francisco Gate*, 2014. https://www.sfgate.com/bayarea/article/When-the-flow-of-traffic-was-all-aboard-the-5923134.php.

Plunkett, Lois Netherton. Interview with Theresa Griffin Kennedy, 2019.

Rick. "River Queen." *Pacific Northwest Photoblog*, 2010. http://pnwphotoblog.com/river-queen.

Roylance, Doug. Interview with Theresa Griffin Kennedy, Oregon, 2019.

Wikipedia. "Six Minute Ferries." Accessed via Wikiwand. https://www.wikiwand.com/en/Six_Minute_ferries.

Der Rheinländer Restaurant

Anderson, Heather Arndt. "Horst Mager: Portland's First Celebrity Chef: An Empire Builder and TV Personality with a Lasting Legacy." Eater, Portland, Oregon, January 28, 2015. https://pdx.eater.com/2015/1/28/7931327/horst-mager-portlands-first-celebrity-chef.

Fox News. "Der Rheinlander in NE Portland to Close Early Next Year, Building Sold to Developer." 2017. https://www.kptv.com/news/der-rheinlander-in-ne-portland-to-close-early-next-year/article_1027d967-4a85-5362-b735-3bd9344cc75e.html.

Guten Foods Inc. "Rhinelander 1963–2016." 2017. https://www.gutenfoods.com/#rheinlander.

Korfhage, Matthew. "Der Rheinlander German Restaurant Is Closing After Over 50 Years." *Willamette Week*, September 27, 2016. https://www.wweek.com/restaurants/2016/09/27/der-rheinlander-german-restaurant-is-closing-after-over-50-years.

Perkins, Ted. "Rhinelander Will Make Way for Portland Clinic—with Parking." *Hollywood Star News*, 2016. http://star-news.info/2016/10/11/rheinlander-will-make-way-for-portland-clinic-with-parking.

Old Wives' Tales Restaurant

Binder, Melissa. "Old Wives' Tales Closes, Building Sold to Apartment Developer; Owner Says Progressive Restaurant 'Outlived Usefulness' (Q&A)." *Oregonian*, 2014. https://www.oregonlive.com/portland/index.ssf/2014/05/old_wives_tales_closes_buildin.html.

Cascadia Kids. "10 Family Friendly Restaurants in Portland." 2010. http://www.cascadiakids.com/family-friendly-restaurants-portland.

Gluten Free Portland. "Restaurant Review: Dessert at Old Wives' Tales." 2009. http://glutenfreeportland.org/2009/03/17/restaurant-review-dessert-at-old-wives-tales.

Hart, Holly. Interview with Theresa Griffin Kennedy, 2021.

Jewish Life Oregon. "Holly Hart Combines Food with Social Activism." 2014. https://orjewishlife.com/holly-hart-combines-food-social-activism.

Nicola, George. "Interview with Holly Hart, One of the Founders of the Gay Liberation Front in Portland, Oregon." *Gay and Lesbian Archives of the Pacific Northwest*, 2000. https://www.glapn.org/6048HollyHartInterview.html.

Ogintz, Eileen. "Taking the Kids for Healthier Meals When Traveling." *Today*, 2013. https://www.today.com/money/taking-kids-healthier-meals-when-traveling-1C8424123.

PDX Food Dude. "Confirmed: Old Wives' Tales Closing May 4th." Portland Food and Drink, 2014. https://portlandfoodanddrink.com/rumor-mill-old-wives-tales-closing-may-4th.

Push the Plate. "Old Wives' Tales." 2013. http://pushtheplate.blogspot.com/2013/02/old-wives-tales.html.

Willamette Week. "Old Wives' Tales Closed After 34 Years: Restaurant Was a Haven for Activists, Vegans, LGBT Community." 2017. https://www.wweek.com/portland/blog-31577-old-wives-tales-closed-after-34-years.html.

Yelp. "Menu for Old Wives' Tales." https://www.yelp.com/menu/old-wives-tales-portland/lunch-menu.

Café Lena

Drake, Monica. "Café Lena." Food and Drink, *Portland Mercury*, 2001. https://www.portlandmercury.com/food/caf-lena/Content?oid=24633.

Grable, Leanne. Interview with Theresa Griffin Kennedy, Oregon, 2019.

Hicks, Bob. "Poetic Justice; Café Lena Cooks Again." Oregon Arts Watch, 2016. http://www.orartswatch.org/poetic-justice-cafe-lena-cooks-again.

Sander, Gina. Interview with Theresa Griffin Kennedy, Oregon, 2021.

Sander, Steve. Interview with Theresa Griffin Kennedy, Oregon, 2019.

Silvas, Steffen. "Change of Scene: Two Popular Cafes, Café Lena and La Patisserie, Have Changed Hand and Style." *Willamette Week*, July 30, 2002. https://www.wweek.com/portland/article-1184-change-of-scene.html.

About the Author

Theresa Griffin Kennedy is a native Portlander with a strong connection to her Pacific Northwest heritage, rooted in the blue-collar, working-class experience. Currently fifty-six years old, she has been writing since the age of eighteen, when her father, Dorsey Edwin Griffin—also a writer, author and poet—began encouraging her to write. Kennedy has been published with *The Rumpus*, *Pathos Literary Review*, *Portland Monthly Magazine*, the *Portland Alliance* and *Street Roots*, with letters to the editor published with the *Portland Tribune*, *Willamette Week* and *Vanity Fair*. She was educated at Portland State University and earned undergraduate and graduate degrees there. Her first book of fiction, *Burnside Field Lizard and Selected Stories*, was selected as a finalist for the 2019 Next Generation Indie Book Award for the regional fiction division. Kennedy continues to live in Portland with her husband, Don DuPay, also a writer and author.